<u>Disclaimer</u>

This manual was diligently researched and compiled with the intent to provide information for persons wishing to learn about Social Networking.

No information provided in this report constitutes a warranty of any kind; nor shall readers of this report rely solely on any such information or advice. All content, products, and services are not to be considered as legal, medical, or professional advice and are to be used for personal use and information purposes only. This manual makes no warranties or guarantees express or implied, as to the results provided by the strategies, techniques, and advice presented in this report. The publishers of this report expressly disclaim any liability arising from any strategies, techniques, and advice presented in this report.

The purpose of this manual is to educate and guide. Neither the publisher nor the author warrant that the information contained within this manual is free of omissions or errors and is fully complete. Furthermore, neither the publisher nor the author shall have responsibility or liability to any entity or person as a result of any damage or loss alleged to be caused or caused indirectly or directly by this manual.

For Educational Use ONLY!

Some of our Other Products on Amazon

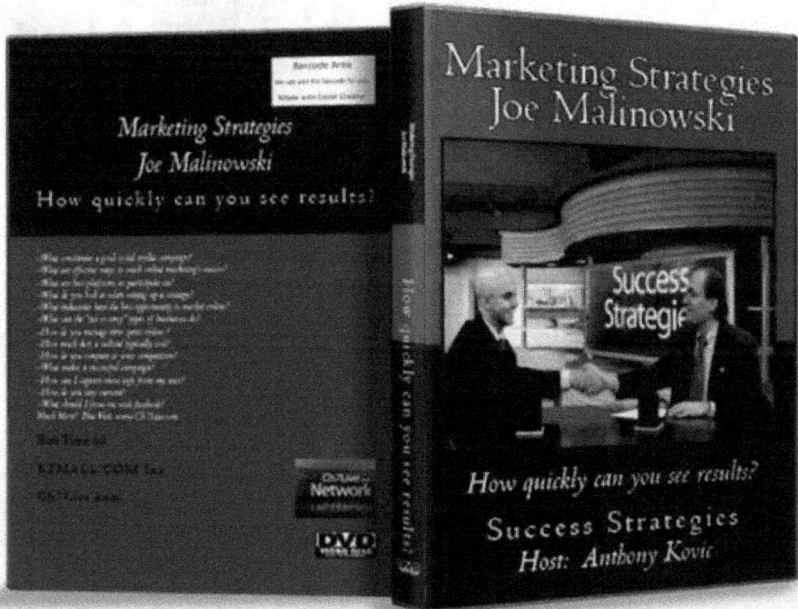

Other DVD Tittles on Amazon Short Link **http://dld.bz/bCcgK**

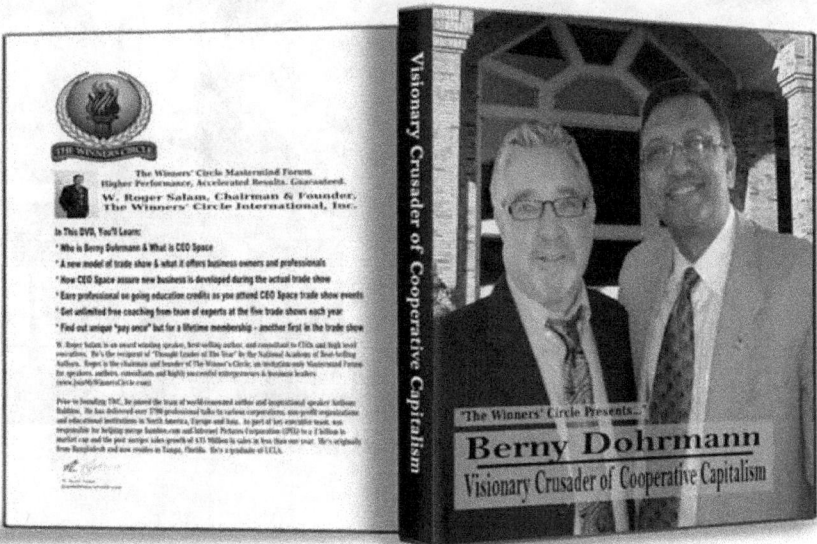

Other DVD Tittles on Amazon Short Link **http://dld.bz/bCwmu**

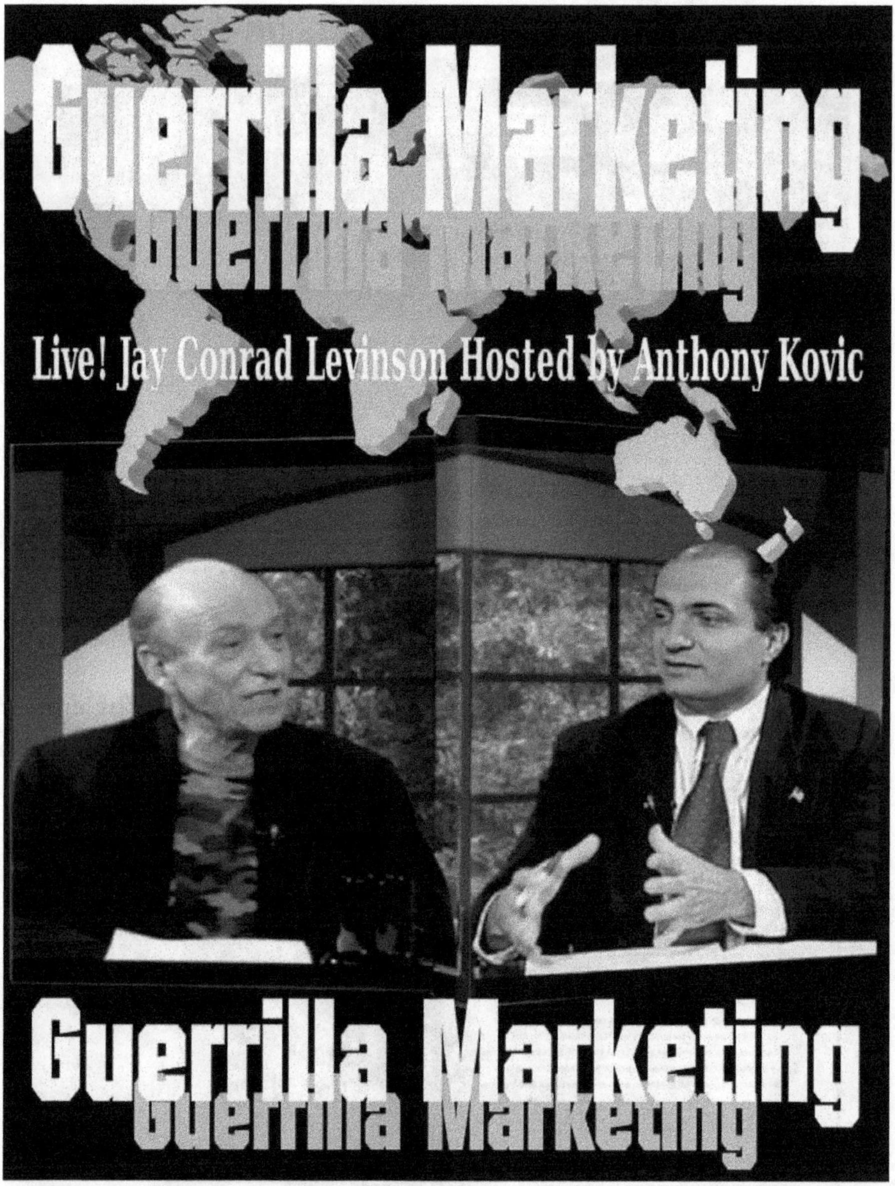

Direct Amazon Link: http://dld.bz/bHGUF

Index

For Amazon Look Inside Preview of this book provides over 340+ Business & Personal Screen Shots with descriptions That the Top Info Marketers Use Samples:

Linkroll.com
This is a social bookmarking service that allows users to save links to their favorite pages and comment on other people's bookmarks.

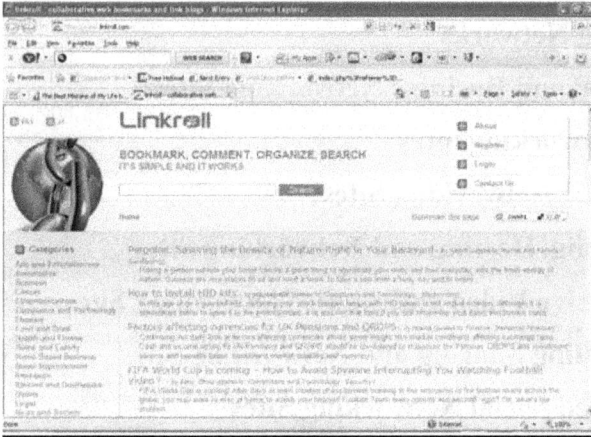

MisterWong.com
This easy to use bookmarking site is integrated with Twitter so that users can automatically import interesting links.

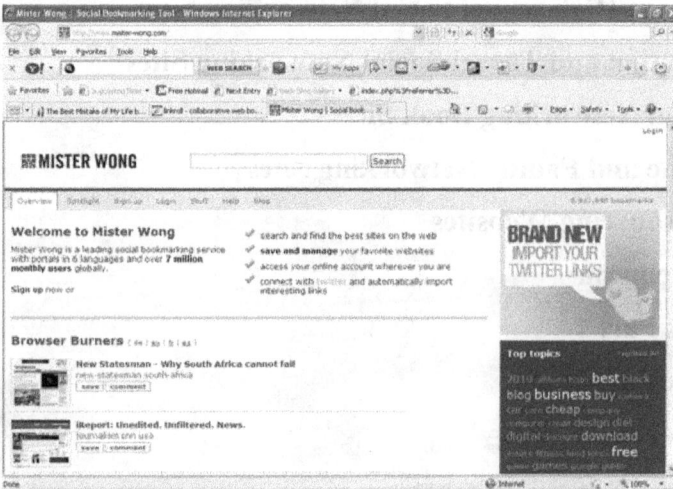

GetACoder.com

The outsourcing website offers users a platform to tap into a global workforce of service providers like programmers, writers, web-designers, etc.

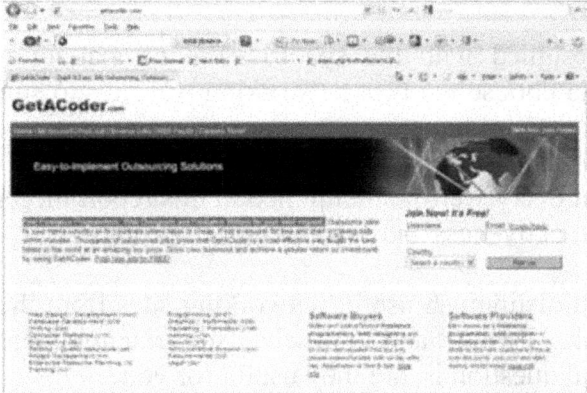

Chillibreeze.com

You can post your writing/editing/content management jobs to this site for free. The site has a user base of Indian providers.

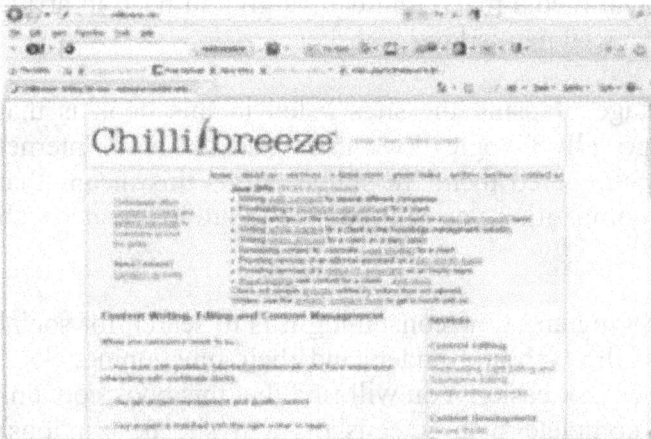

End Sample Preview

Introduction

A Resource Guide Of The Top Social Networking Sites for 2012', is the most comprehensive list of the most useful Social Networking Sites, that you'll find anywhere on the web.

This book has been designed with the specific aim of making it simpler for the readers to choose the best networking websites to suit their business and social networking requirements.

You can rest assured that every website mentioned in this report meets high standards of quality, activeness and search engine friendliness.

This guide will help you distinguish useful networking sites from the popular ones. Facebook, Twitter and Youtube, for example, are popular sites, but the vital question is, are they useful for you?

There is no denying the fact that these sites can help you reach out to a huge customer base, but the problem is that focusing on only the 'popular' sites will put you in a situation where your efforts and rewards will not be proportional.

For a successful social media marketing campaign you need to arrive at the right 'mix' of social networking websites.

The biggest advantage of using the sites listed in this book is that search engines (especially Google) love them and yet most internet marketers haven't discovered them! In simple terms this means that despite facing less competition you will be able to attract greater web traffic.

I understand how boring and time consuming it is to search for social networking sites on the web and understand their functioning. So, I decided to make your task easier. You will find that this book contains hundreds of sites (complete with screenshots and site descriptions) sorted into different categories. The purpose of doing the same was not to overwhelm you with information, but to help you, understand the key functions of each website so that you can pick out the ones that you feel will serve your needs best.

For instance, if you want to design a social media marketing campaign for your online fashion house, you may want concentrate on the sites in the- Social shopping, niche specific networking websites, family networking websites and high school/college networking sections, as it is here that you are likely to find people who will fit into your target market.

It's important to remember that you don't have to use all the websites in the categories of your choice, unless you have a big staff at your disposal. My advice to you is that you should concentrate on six or seven from this book that you feel are easy to use and will suit your networking needs. You will realize that in the long run building good networks on a few high traffic generating sites is a better option than building average networks on several websites!

I have designed this manual in such a way that by the time you have finished reading it you will have gained a clearer understanding of the key concepts of internet marketing and would have amassed enough practical knowledge about social media to leverage it for greater profits.

Chapter 1

Web 2.0 Explained

Web 2.0 is a term used to describe applications that bring together like minded users and facilitate information sharing, collaboration and various other forms of online interaction.

Web 2.0 based websites organize and categorize information on basis of keywords and tags, thus making it easier for users to search and find specific information. Social networking, social bookmarking, wikis, video sharing, blogs, media sharing networks, etc, all come under the gambit of Web 2.0 applications.

Web 2.0 and Internet Marketing

Web 2.0 applications can serve as your personal marketing research department. After all, the applications perform essentially the same tasks-filtering information on consumers and consolidating demographic information

Web 2.0 applications provide marketers with a platform where they can interact freely with their customers/clients. Consumers in fact voluntarily share information about their preferences, tastes and demands on Web 2.0 based websites, giving marketers an opportunity to gather valuable data at a minimal cost.

So, as a marketer you can use social media to-

- Segment and augment the market- By monitoring social networks that you are a part of and using their search features you can easily narrow down your target market.

- Build your brand value- By interacting with customers and sharing valuable information you can give a likeable face to your business. Your customers will start connecting with you and associating the positive qualities that you project with your business.

- Understand your customers' mindset- By interacting directly

with your customers you will be able to understand their demands, needs and requirements better.

- Monitor and track the performance of your products and services- Instead of conducting huge and expensive surveys, you can gauge customer reaction directly by using social media.

- Expand your customer base- Content submitted to social networking websites gets a lot of visibility by riding on their popularity. This means that you can tap into a huge market by using the social networking platform.

- Reduce your marketing expenses- Most social media websites are either free to use or charge a nominal joining fee. You can either manage your marketing campaign yourself or hire people to do it. Even if you do the latter the cost involved will be far less than organizing huge marketing activities and programs, like conducting surveys, sending out newsletters, direct or door-to-door marketing, etc.

- Gain more profits- Through social media you can target specific customer groups who have voluntarily expressed their need for the kind of products and services you offer.

How to develop Great Content

Great content is the key to the success of a social media marketing campaign. It is the content (articles, videos, blogs, posts, podcasts, music files, photos, etc) that you post on the web that will help you grab eye balls and pull traffic to your website. The vital question now is- what exactly constitutes great content? Great content simply is something that can attract the visitors to your site. This means that it should be-

Well researched

Making tall claims in your articles/videos/podcasts or using false or unverified information won't impress any users. It will in fact backfire on your business. So, check and cross check your facts before uploading anything online.

Relevant

Putting together a string of keywords or filling your articles with SEO junk will not win you any brownie points with social networking websites. The content that you post must be relevant and of high quality, only then can you hope to gain any mileage out of it.

Use the right keywords

There are lots of free tools online that allow you to research for keywords. Using extremely popular keywords may sound tempting but it is not the best idea, as it would mean greater competition. If you do some research you will notice that generic keywords are the most popular ones, it is therefore a good idea to focus on your niche area while choosing keywords.

For example, if you run an online fashion store, you should avoid using generic keywords like fashion, style, etc; instead you should focus on niche areas like plus size, lingerie, camisoles, etc. Using niche keywords will help direct those users to your websites who are looking for the very items specified through the keywords. What's more, since competition in such keywords is likely to be less, your content will get better search engine ratings.

Write a compelling opening and a creative headline

If you are posting an article or a blog, your opening must draw the reader in. Most people decide after reading the first few lines, whether they want to stay on that page or move to the next. Remember all it takes for a user to navigate off your page is a simple mouse click. So, you have to catch people's attention with your opening paragraph. The same rule applies to videos too; your intro should be impressive and persuasive.

The best way to do this is to think like 'the user'. Ask yourself what would you have liked to read if you were looking for information on the subject you are writing on? For instance, if you are writing a factual blog or article on symptoms of pregnancy, a flowery beginning about the joys of motherhood won't do you much good. On the other hand if you start your article with the most likely question on the users mind, you have a better chance of grabbing their attention. Something like-

"Feeling nauseous, fatigued or constantly hungry? Wondering if they are actually the symptoms you are looking or just a false alarm? Then read on..."

Would probably work well for you.

Add bookmarking options to your webpage/blog

You want people to bookmark your page, right? Well, then make it easy for them and add bookmark icons to your webpage. You can do this by- pasting a simple HTML code, add bookmarks individually from each social bookmarking site, or by running simple scripts that will add multiple buttons in one go. You can find a great one on this website

http://addtobookmarks.com/

Make good use of tags

A tag really is a relevant keyword or term that is used to describe a particular piece of content. Usually each chunk of information has more than one tag associated with it.

Most websites use tags to categorize information, so that users can find what they are looking for easily.

One question that I am asked most often is about the difference between categories and tags.

Tags are more specific than categories, also most websites offer several features associated with tags that can make it easier for readers to find the exact information that they are looking for. Let's say you sell holiday packages and your website has categories like- Adventure holidays, Romantic breaks, Mini-breaks, Budget holidays, etc. Now a particular visitor is looking for information about California on your blog, if you have created location tags, it will be easy for this visitor to click on that tag and view all posts about California. You can also use the 'dual plug in' option, so that when a reader clicks on a keyword (that you have used to tag the article as well), he is taken to the page that contains all your posts related to the tag/keyword.

Social networking gives a personal touch to business. As you post more high quality content on the net, join relevant networks and build your community, more people will start to associate with you. In effect your brand value will improve, your customer base will increase and so will your profit margin.

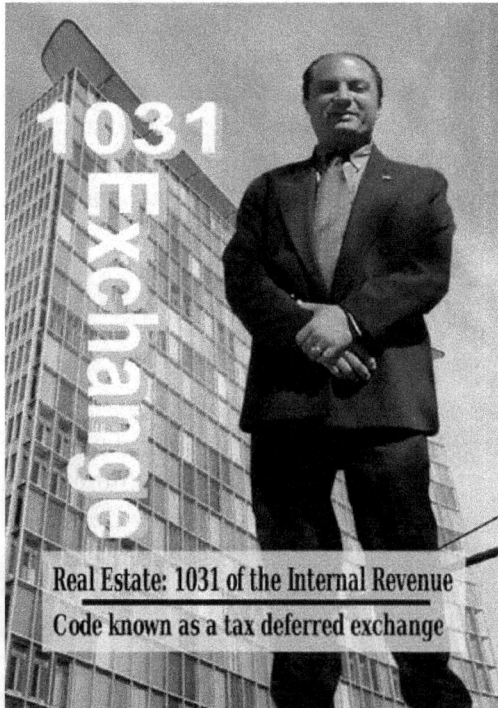

Real Estate: 1031 of the Internal Revenue Code known as a tax deferred exchange

Direct Amazon Short Link **http://dld.bz/bCaYw**

Chapter 2

Social Bookmarking and Social Media

You like a website or find a particular piece of information extremely useful, so you bookmark it for later use. Thousands others like you also do the same whenever they come across information that they find useful and/or interesting- when you put these virtual bookmarks together you have a treasure trove of information! That's what social bookmarking is all about.

Social bookmarking networks started as way to share information categorized on the basis of certain keywords. The purpose of such networks was to make it easier for their members to look for information that they wanted without having to sift through pages and pages of junk.

Marketers soon discovered that they could actually use these networks to promote their businesses and thus started the wave of marketing to through social bookmarking sites.

Social Bookmarking Marketing

Any content posted on a social bookmarking site has the potential to be read by millions of people, as these sites attract regular high traffic. So, essentially as a marketer you get a free platform to show off you wares to a huge customer base!

The other advantage of posting your content on a social bookmarking website is that it will help in improving your site's search engine ratings. All search engines (including Google) value back-links (references to your site on other sites) and posting relevant or interesting content with a link leading back to your website will help in improving its search engine positioning.

In fact if your information is truly interesting or useful, other members of the social bookmarking network may bookmark your site, thereby increasing its popularity.

For instance, in the social bookmarking network Digg.com users can rate and post

their comments on articles, videos and podcasts on several different topics. The most popular items are posted on the website's front page. The rest are placed in the logs for the network's members to view and rate. Thanks to its huge membership and search engine popularity, content posted on Digg.com has the potential to be seen by thousands of users and if it makes to the front page, you will have hit jackpot! Of course for your content to find its way to the coveted position, it must be of relevance to Digg's readers.

How to use social bookmarking sites

The important thing about social bookmarking is that the marketing strategy you adopt needs to be very subtle, i.e. it must seem like you are on the website to share information and not to promote your business.

The first thing that you need to do therefore is to create a genuine profile, with a valid e-mail address. Though all social bookmarking sites are designed differently, they generally allow users to access their features, post comments, add bookmarks and build their own pages, after they have registered themselves.

Building your Identity

Apart from sharing content most people use social bookmarking sites to build their unique identities on the net and interact with others who share their interests. For marketers, this is one of the most important aspects of social bookmarking.

Building you own identity will help you build your personal and professional goodwill and through your interactions with other members of the community you can gather important information about-

- Consumer/customer behavior trends
- Personal preferences of your target customers/consumers

- New products/services in your niche area
- The merits and flaws of the products and services marketed by your competitors; etc

How to create and maintain your profile?

Your profile should not be too businesslike or formal. Remember the purpose of building your profile is to connect with other users. This means your profile should not make people feel that you are on the website only to serve your business interests.

Choose an interesting screen name that says something about your personality or stick to using your actual name. You may post a picture if you feel comfortable with idea; it will make your profile appear more credible.

The next step is to upload links to your website and if the site allows you may also write a little note about your products and services.

In order to build your popularity in the network, you must stay active, interact with other users, post reviews and comments frequently, create and participate in discussions and expand your network by adding new people to your contact list.

Staying active on social bookmarking websites in fact also offers the added advantage of tapping into the collective intelligence of the network, so that you can gain a better understanding of your target customer/consumer's demands and preferences.

How to make yours site conductive to Social Media?

If you want to gain the maximum mileage from Social Media, you must make your website conductive to it. This means that your website should essentially have the following features-

➤ The content should be SEO friendly. In social media websites, content is sorted by keywords or tags. These tags help users find websites that contain information on the same subject. So, by making your content SEO-friendly, you'll make it easier for users to locate your website.

➢ Consider embedding relevant videos on your site. This will give you the added advantage of building your web-presence on social networks dedicated to sharing videos.

➢ Add informational blogs to your site. To use social media to your advantage you must post content that is of relevance to a network's members. By adding informational blogs to your website, you will be able to generate more traffic as people will click on your content for its informational value.

➢ Create a link wheel with your articles. Links wheeling is a technique that involves creating articles related to your main business website and then posting them to web 2.0 sites. The articles should focus on a targeted keyword, so in effect each article becomes a spoke and your main website acts as a hub. Each article that you write should be unique but related to the other articles. For instance, if you are in the business of selling online gadgets, you can create 'How to' shopping articles about the gadgets available in your online store and link them all to your primary site. By categorizing them in the same genre you create a link between your articles. Since 'How to' articles are bound to be informational there is a good chance that people will click on the link to your website for more information after reading them. The following diagram will perhaps make this concept clearer to you.

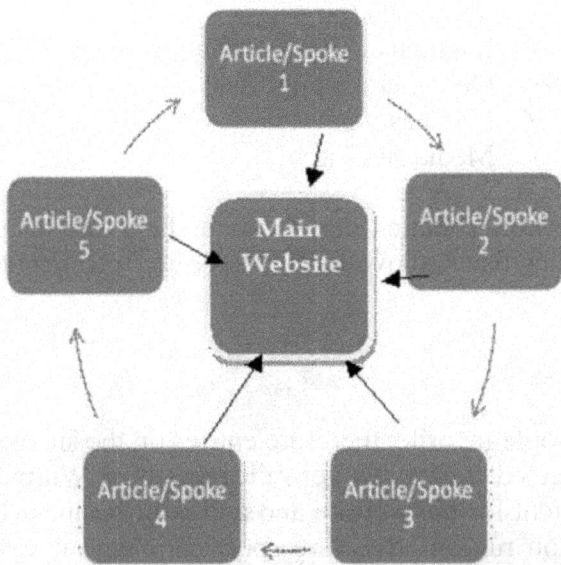

Diagram-The link wheel

> You can add another dimension to your links wheel by creating back links to each of the spokes (read articles), through social bookmarking, blog commenting, forum posting, etc.

> Model your website in such a way that it can at least use two or three of the most popular social media technologies to boost traffic. Here is a list of some of the most popular social media options that you must take into account while designing your website.

Wikipedia

- ✓ Social networking communities
- ✓ Video sharing
- ✓ Interactive sites focusing on events
- ✓ Online audio episodes
- ✓ Live casting
- ✓ Media sharing

The following section contains details about how you can use the social media options listed above to direct greater web traffic to your website.

How to use Wikipedia

Wikipedia is a Google favorite; therefore entries on the site get a lot of search engine directed traffic. To get mileage out of Wikipedia, you should create content for the website and add your business-link to it. For instance, if you run an adventure sport company, it would be a good idea to create travel related content about your town, add you business link to the article and post it on Wikipedia/Wikitravel.

Wikipedia articles are often bookmarked by a lot of users. So, if your content is interesting and informational, there is a good chance that the page will get bookmarked and you will get an opportunity to attract even more web traffic.

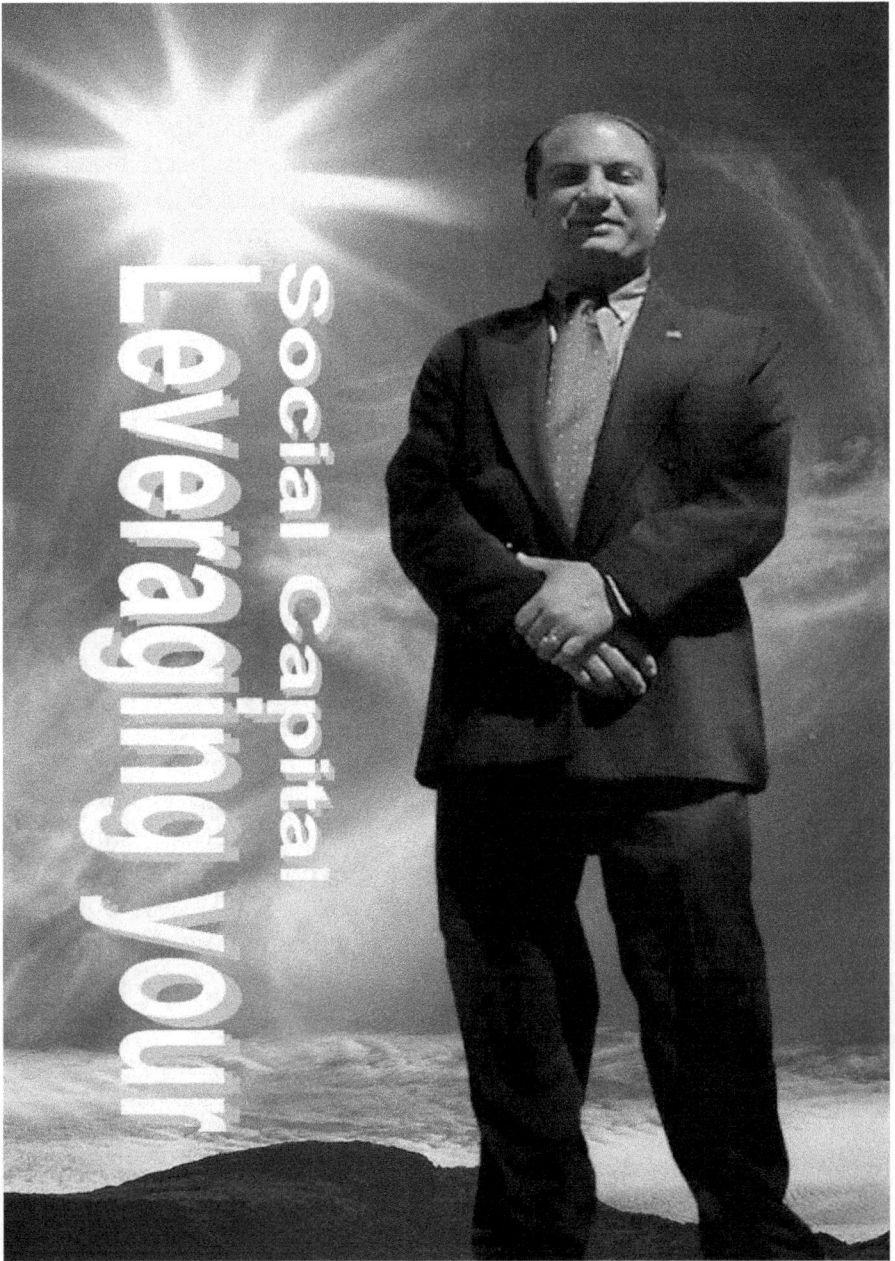

Direct Amazon.com Short Link **http://dld.bz/bCaWX**

How to use Social Networking Sites

You can use Social networking websites to interact directly with your customers, improve your goodwill and get an insight into their demands and requirements. Sites like LinkedIn, Myspace, Facebook, etc, encourage casual interaction between its members. You can take advantage of this and get to know your customer base better. For example, you may post your opinion on a new kind of technology in your industry on Facebook and encourage a discussion on it or a post a link to an interesting article related to the niche area you operate in and encourage your contacts to comment on it. Through such interactions, not only will you be able to build your brand presence, but will also be able to understand your customers' needs and expectations better.

How to use Video Sites?

Video sharing networks are fast gaining popularity. To cash on the success of video blogging and networking sites, it would be a smart move to create interesting, unique and informative videos in order to encourage people to visit your website. For example, if you run a financial consultancy business, you may create small videos giving out general money management and stock market investing tips. These videos will not only help in building your brand value, but will also encourage people to visit your website and seek out your services. The better the content of your video, the more chances there are that it will be bookmarked.

How to use Interactive sites focusing on events

Events and new innovations have news value. By posting press releases of events that you plan to organize as a part of your marketing efforts or articles about your latest user friendly innovations, you can get a lot of exposure and attention.

Creating content about new trends or notable events in your area of operation can help you find favor with popular social bookmarking communities like pinterest, technocrati, reddit, digg, etc.

How to use Podcasts?

Just like videos, podcasts can also help you attract greater traffic to your website. What you need to do is to create relevant and interesting audio content, related to your business, embed it on your website and post it on social bookmarking sites as well.

A lot of people prefer listening to content than reading it and sites like digg and technocrati even have sections dedicated to podcasts/audio files.

How to use Livecasts?

Livecasts are online events that people can join in irrespective of their geographical location. The advantage of organizing online live events is that they are cheaper to organize (as compared to real world events) but promise better exposure. You can also print press releases highlighting the event and distribute them through press release submission and distribution websites to create a buzz in the online world.

Media Sharing

Media sharing networks allow its users to upload, compress, distribute and share pictures, text, applications, games, music, videos, etc. These networking sites too can be used to build your brand image and expand your network.

You may choose the social media sharing technology that you are most comfortable with. The key is to create high quality content so that you can build a consistent and valuable presence in different social media outlets.

Chapter 3

Choosing the right plan of attack to use social networking for traffic generation

How to choose your networks?
To choose the right social network, you should take the following facts into consideration-

- What kind of networks would you be comfortable using?

- What networks are the most closely associated with you area of interest/niche?

- Whether or not networks you have chosen have a high level of user activity?

- How popular are they among the search engines?

- Which part of the world are most of the network users based in?

Your comfort level will depend on your skills and budget. If you can produce videos on your own or pay someone to produce and edit them for you, then you can easily join video sharing websites. Similarly, if you are comfortable creating articles or have the resources to hire someone to do the same, you shouldn't have a problem joining blog networks.

This means that you have to decide which media you are most comfortable working with and choose your social networks accordingly.

Joining the networks closest to your niche area can lead you straight to a huge market of potential customers. If you can find a network based on your area of operation, then you don't have to look too far! It is like almost getting customers on a platter.

However, it isn't necessary to find an exact match in terms of networks and your niche area. With a little research you can easily identify networks with user bases that can fit into your target market. For instance, if you sell gadgets, you should consider joining young entrepreneur networks, sports based networks and even some general social networking sites. On the other hand, if you sell beauty products, you would probably do well in student networks, women's networks, fashion/lifestyle based groups and social shopping networks.

It is also important for a network to have high user activity, networks with a huge user base, won't do your business much good, unless the users are active and loyal. After all you join a social network to interact with its members so that you can convert them into customers, right? But, you won't be able to do either of the two things if the users aren't available online!

Search engine popularity is another key factor. If the social network you have joined has high search engine ratings, you are likely to gain more benefit from it by riding on its popularity.

Finally, if the geographical location of the users is important to your business, then you must choose from networks based in your area of operation.

So, you have chosen your network, what next?

Once you have zeroed in on the networks, you can launch your attack. The following are some steps that I strongly recommend-

<u>Read the community guidelines carefully</u> before you start posting your content/bookmarks or interacting with other members. Violating the TOS of a network can get you banned and that will certainly not be good for your brand image.

<u>Post interesting information about the niche area</u> that the website is based on and make sure that the post doesn't sound too promotional.

<u>Participate in the discussions and online activities</u> on the website to expand your network.

Comment on other people's posts and status updates. The more active you stay, the better your brand image will be.

Organize discussions and online activities on your own and encourage people participation to increase your goodwill.

Post interesting pictures, videos or whatever media files the website allows users to post to make your profile page interesting. The better the content of your profile, the more the number of visitors you will be able to attract.

Organize online events and post notifications about it on your profile to create a buzz about your organization.

Social gaming is also an excellent way to build contacts. Most networks have some social games that users can play. You can also join social gaming networks to expand your contacts, if you feel that the members of such websites can fit into your target market.

How to build links?

Back links are a natural by-product of creating bookmarks on social networking website. However, if you want to gain the maximum mileage out of these sites, you should try the following as well-

- Include your link as a tag on your profile name.
- Comment on blogs, posts and links posted by other members and provide a back link to your website, if it is relevant to your comment.
- Copy and paste links to the new information that you have posted on relevant discussion boards.
- If html is allowed in the comments section, draft your comment in such a way that you can slip in your business keyword (embedded with your weblink) into it.
- Embed weblinks in your pictures or leave links to your website below your videos/pictures.

Through these additional link building activities you will be able to improve your search engine's ratings as well as your business's web presence.

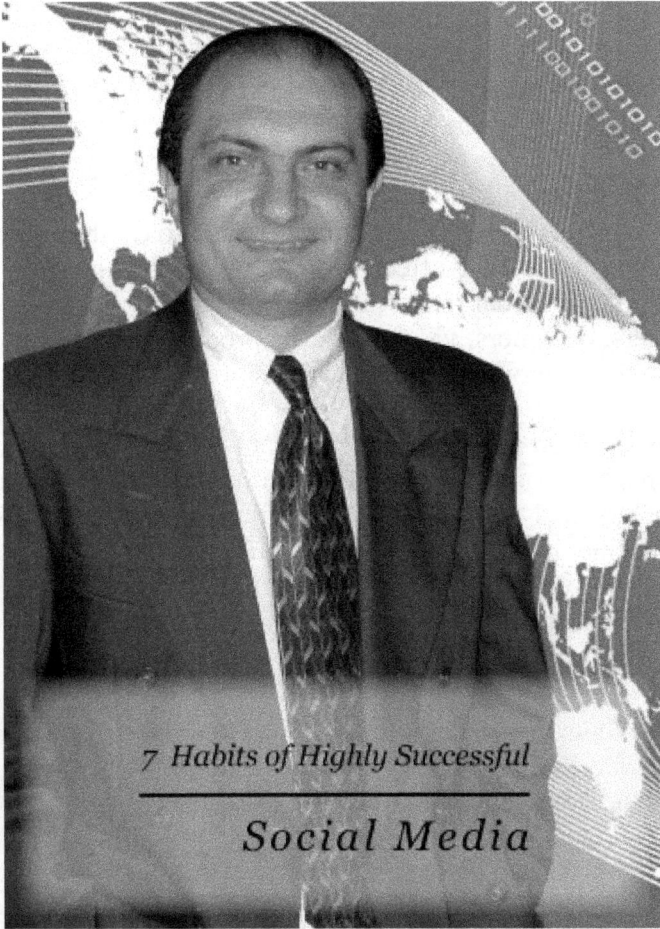

7 Habits of Highly Successful

Social Media

Amazon Direct Link: **http://dld.bz/bCba9**

Chapter 4

Outsourcing Networks

So, far I have told you the importance of uploading high quality content, interacting with other users, creating back-links, managing your profile and gathering market data from social networking websites. Now I wouldn't be surprised if you are already shaking your head and wondering, "Just how am I going to do all this?"

The good news is that **you don't have to**! No you do not need to invest in an office space and hire a huge staff to do the work for you. That would kill the cost effectiveness of social marketing. You can instead tap into a global market of talented writers, internet marketers, programmers, designers, video/podcasts producers/editors and website developers through outsourcing networks.

The fact is that you are the most important part of your business, so to use your resources most efficiently you must focus on the tasks that need your personal attention and outsource the rest to others. Now, I understand that if you have been handling most of your business processes on your own, this decision may be difficult to take. However, if you break down your entire process into simple tasks it would be easier for you to figure out-

> ➢ Which tasks you need to focus on personally?

> ➢ What tasks can be automated?

> ➢ What tasks can be outsourced?

For instance, let's say you sell sports goods online. Now if you break down your online marketing business process into small simple tasks it would probably look something like this-

> ➢ Website marketing-Back link creation, e-books, social media interaction, media creation and posting.

> ➢ Advertising and promotion-Identify websites, get in touch with ad sales departments, place ads.

➢ Ad tracking.

➢ Public and media relations-Draft press releases, send them to media houses, manage media relations.

➢ Email marketing-create newsletters, procure mailing lists, send e-mails, handle responses.

An objective examination of these tasks will help you figure out that your personal involvement is needed at the planning and supervisory level only. You can outsource or automate the mundane/routine tasks.

In website marketing for example, you can draft the outline of the e-books you want to create, zero in on the social media websites that can help you meet your business goals and design your social media interaction activities. The job of executing these tasks can be left to skilled freelancers.

Even in e-mail marketing some tasks like drafting emails/newsletters can be outsourced and others like sending e-mails and auto-responders can be automated.

What you need to do is to examine each task of your business process and ask yourself- How much time will it save me if I delegate or automate this task? What can I do to develop my business if I do not have to worry about these tasks? The answers will help you make the right outsourcing decision.

At the end of the day you want your business to bring you profits. Outsourcing can help improve your overall efficiency so that you can use your vision and expertise for business development and expansion.

How do Outsourcing Websites Work?

The process of hiring through outsourcing websites is simple. Most of them will ask you to register with a valid e-mail address and verify your payment method. Some websites may ask you to pay a nominal joining fee. Once your registration formalities are complete, you can post your job and start interviewing candidates.

As far as your costs are concerned, these sites collect their commissions from the providers, so as a buyer you only have to pay for the amount of work that the selected provider does for you.

Outsourcing websites either ask buyers to deposit payment in an escrow account or act as the middle agents by collecting payments from the buyer and forwarding them to the service provider. Buyers usually have to pay through credit/debit cards.

There are different checks to ensure that buyers are protected. For instance, some websites offer a feature through which you can view the number of hours that the provider has worked along with the screenshots of his/her work, while others give buyers the option of withholding payment if they are not satisfied with the work.

What kind of jobs can you outsource?

Outsourcing websites can literally bring the world to your finger tips, allowing you to take advantage of the skill set of a work force in a far away country at a minimal cost!

Outsourcing websites can basically be divided into three categories-

Niche Specific- These websites give buyers access to providers with certain skill sets like programming, internet marketing, etc.

White collar skilled workforce- These websites have a user base of providers who possess skills like writing, marketing, designing, programming, advertising, editing, etc.

General Outsourcing- Here you can outsource any kind of job as long as it is legal and does not violate the terms and conditions of the website.
So, whether you want someone to –

- ➢ Write high quality SEO blogs and articles for you
- ➢ Manage your blogs and website
- ➢ Create back-links
- ➢ Market your products or website on the internet
- ➢ Build and manage your social media profile
- ➢ Expand your network
- ➢ Build your website or re-design it so that it is more conductive to social media applications
- ➢ Create and distribute press releases
- ➢ Produce videos and/or podcasts
- ➢ Design your ad and marketing campaign
- ➢ Develop software codes
- ➢ Create various media applications
- ➢ Ghostwrite e-books or any other web-content for you
- ➢ Write newsletters or sales copies
- ➢ Handle you data entry system
- ➢ Work as your virtual assistant, etc, you can easily find a skilled provider to do the tasks for you, on of these websites.

What makes outsourcing your work truly cost-effective is that you have the option of choosing the right candidate from a huge global pool. This means that the competition among providers is intense, so you get the best price! You can sit the US and hire a provider from a developing country (and pay less) without leaving the comfort of your home or office.

Chapter 5

Professional and Business Networking Websites

As the name suggests his section contains a list of websites that can help you expand your professional and business network. So, whether you are-

➢ Looking at improving your brand image to enhance your career prospects in the job market

➢ Aiming to build new contacts to expand your client base

➢ Looking for like-minded individuals to share information about your niche area

➢ Aiming to build your websites or product's brand image; you will find the following sites useful.

LinkedIn.com

This is one of the most popular business networking websites on the net with millions of members. Sign up to Linkedin is free.

Go Big Network.com

This is a popular community that helps new and aspiring entrepreneurs connect with investors. Registration to the network is free; however, users have to pay for using premium services.

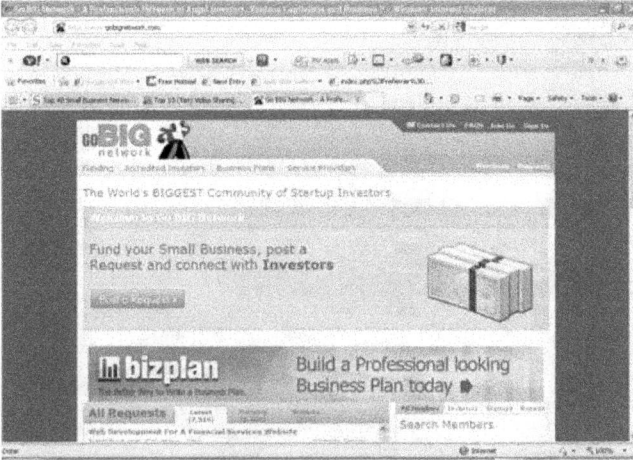

Ryze.com

This is a networking community where you can make new business contacts and stay in touch with your friends. Membership is free.

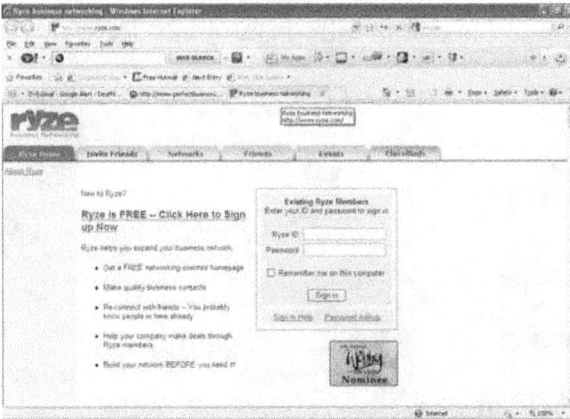

The Warrior Forum.com

The Warrior Forum is one of the most popular Internet Marketing forums on the internet. The website provides a platform for users to discuss debate and brainstorm over internet marketing, money making, self-improvement and various other business related issues. Registration to the website is currently free.

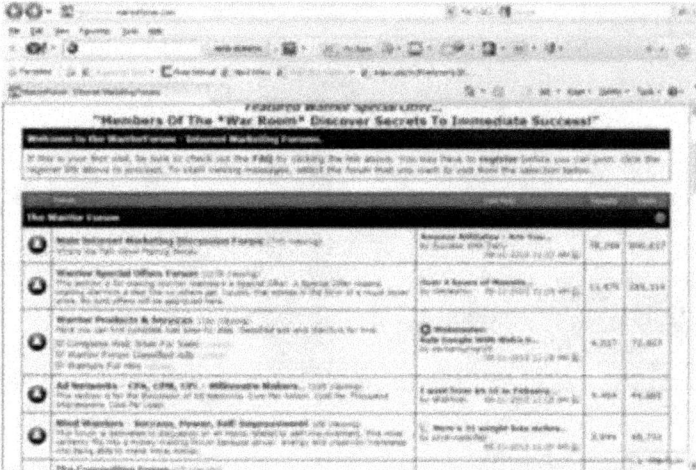

PartnerUp.com

The website is a network of small business owners and entrepreneurs. Membership to the community is currently free.

Biznik.com

The website is an award winning community of small business owners and entrepreneurs. The basic membership to the site is free, premium and pro VIP memberships that offer value added services like video profiles and more visibility cost $10 and $24 respectively.

Confoundr.com

This is a community of startups founders, investors, developers, advisors, CEOs, programmers, and designers. Membership to the website is currently free.

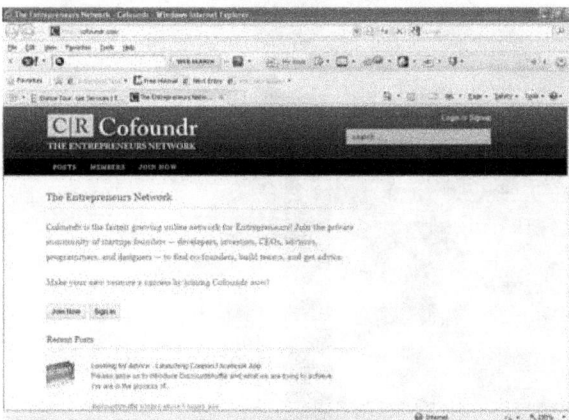

E.Factor.com

This community is designed by entrepreneurs and for entrepreneurs. Membership to this community is free.

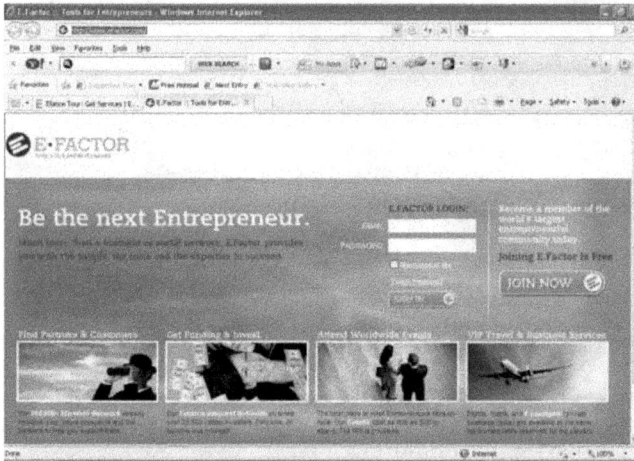

The Funded.com

This is an online community of entrepreneurs to research, review and rate funding sources worldwide. Membership is free for CEOs; others have to pay a joining fee.

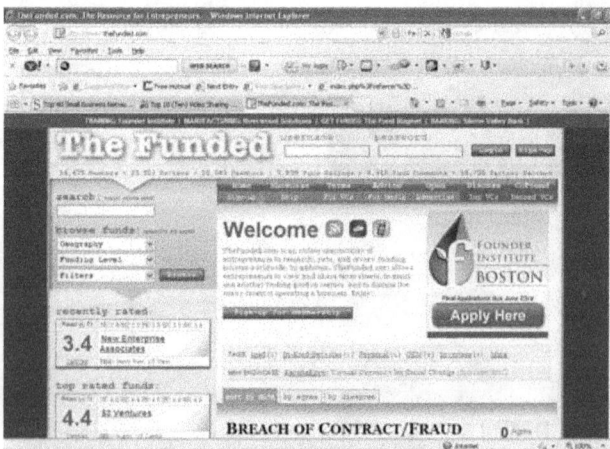

Upspring.com

This online comminity provides users a platform for business networking, local advertising, local Internet marketing, product promotion, and online marketing. Basic membership to Upspring is free, premium services, however, are chargeable.

Affluence.Org

This is a private social network where wealthy individuals connect and share information. Membership to affluence is free but users are required to submit a proof of minimum household net worth of $3 million.

ArtBreak.com

This is a tightly knit community that allows members to buy and sell and art. Membership to this website is free.

Ecademy.com

The website is a community of business people and allows them to share their knowledge, expand their network and build their business. The membership is free.

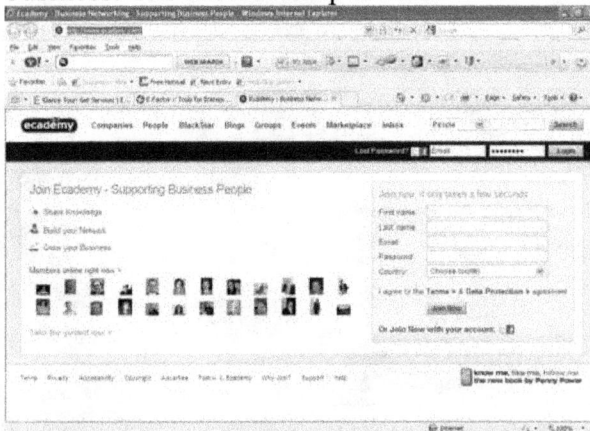

Entrepreneur Connect
www.econnect.entrepreneur.com

It's a community where entrepreneurs can connect with each other. The membership is free.

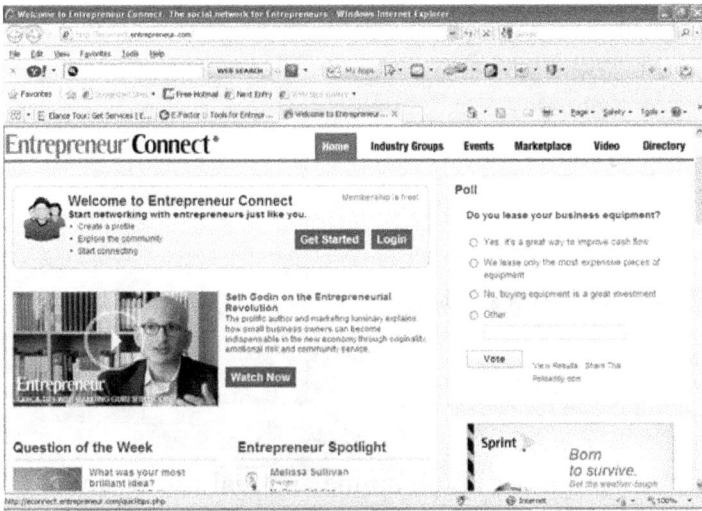

Focus.com

The website is a community of business and technology experts. Membership to this social networking website is free.

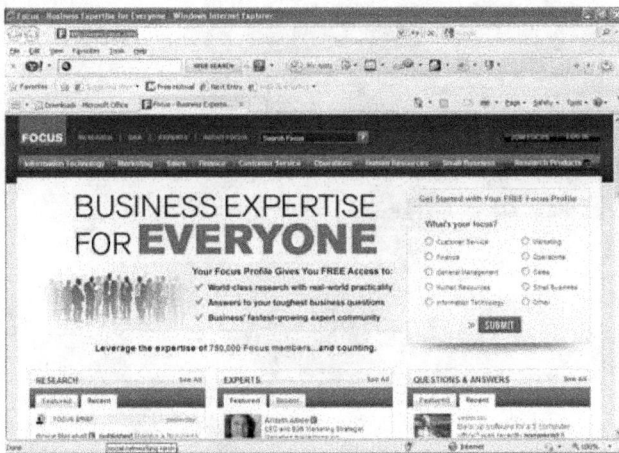

JASEzone.com

This is a network where you can find potential clients and business partners. Membership to the community is free.

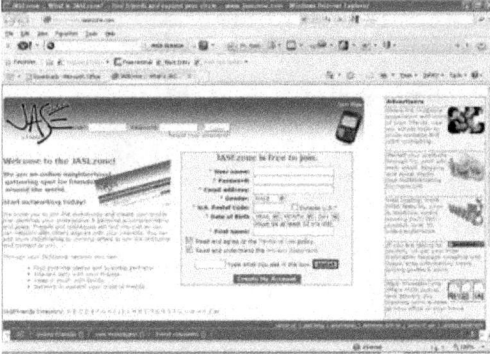

Networking for Professionals.com

The US based website organizes both online and real life business networking events. Membership for the first month is free, subsequently you have to pay $20-$10 depending upon the state you reside in.

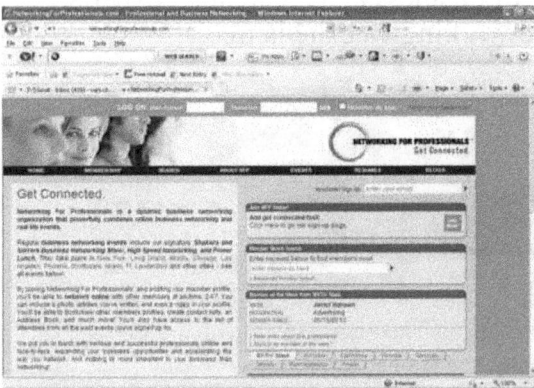

PerfectBusiness.com

The website is a network of enterpreneurs, business experts and investors. Joining this community can help you find investors to launch your business. Membership is free.

Plaxo.com

This is an online address book that can help you manage your other networks. It tracks feeds from networks like Facebook, twitter, etc, so that you can find all your network updates in one place. Membership is free.

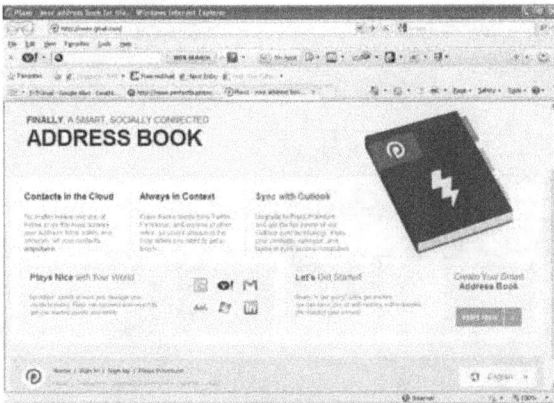

StartupNation.com

This a network formed by entrepernurs and for entreprenurs. Members can exchange ideas, information to help each other achieve entreprenuial success. You can join this community free.

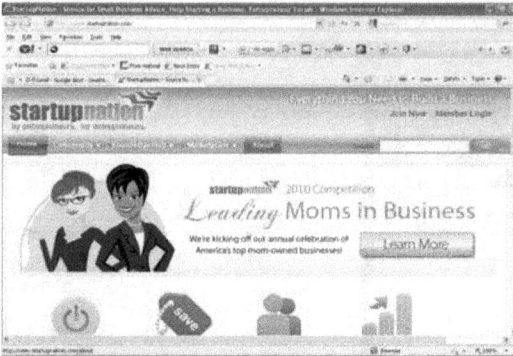

XING.com

It is a prominent European business network with 9 million members. Membership to the community is free.

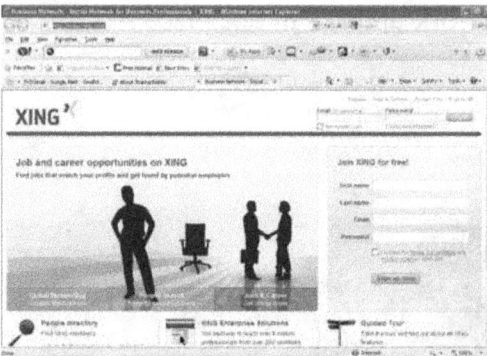

Young Entrepreneur.com

This website is a community of small business and start-up owners , mentors, investors and aspiring entreprenuers. All members can post to the forums by registering for free, however for additional benefits like exchanging private messages, access to premium member forums , you have to buy a gold or platinum membership.

Ziggs.com

The website allows members to build their online brand, market themselves and expand their network. Membership to the community is free.

Blogtronix.com

This pay to use website builds highly specialized tailored communities for large organizations.

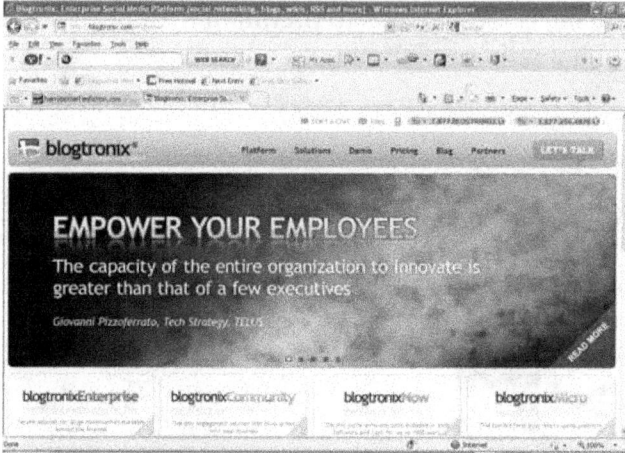

Connect Beam.com

The websites facilitates intra-company networking. The application software that allows companies to connect their employees via the connectbeam network is available at $29. Hardware costs are additional.

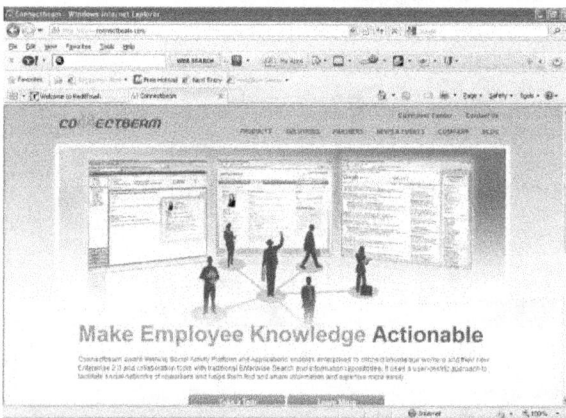

Decorati.com

The website allows interior decorators to network with each other and find clients; they can also buy and sell their products on the website. Membership to Decorati is free, however if you want to avail premium services like receiving client leads before others, greater visibility and the option of putting pictures in your portfolio, you will have a membership fee of $15 per month.

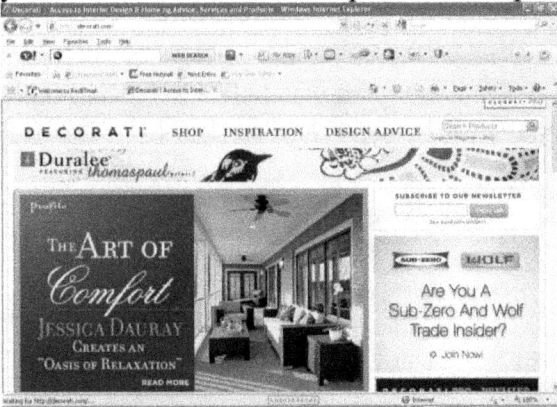

iKarma Inc..com

The networking websites provides reputation and customer feedback systems to business owners and professionals. Membership to iKarma is free.

Imagekind.com

The community faciliates buying, selling and creating artworks.
Memership to Imagekind is free.

Jigsaw.com

The site allows members to create virtual business cards and
exchange them with others, in effect giving everyone access to a
huge database of business owners and professionals. Membership to
Jigsaw is free.

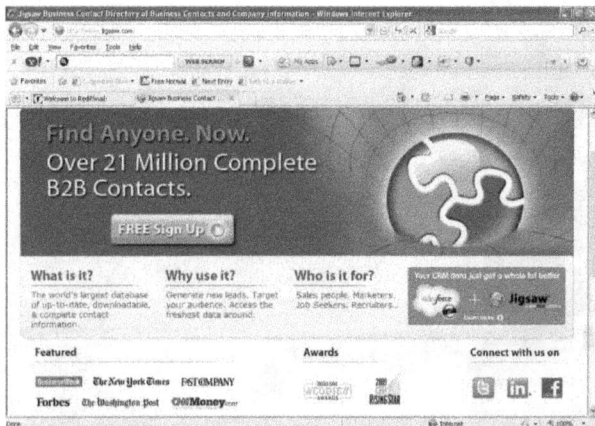

Konnects.com

The site is a social media platform for magazines and newspapers. It allows them to engage their readers and connect with them better. Sign up to Konnects is free.

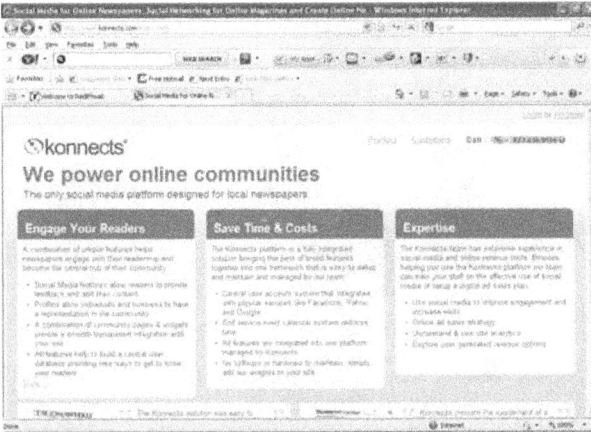

Mediabistro.com

This is a networking site for media professionals. You can register to Mediabistro for free.

Spoke.com

This is a networking website for busines professionals. Sign up to Spoke.com is free.

Vsocial.com

Vsocial is a pay to use service that allows marketers to integrate social media into their marketing campaign.

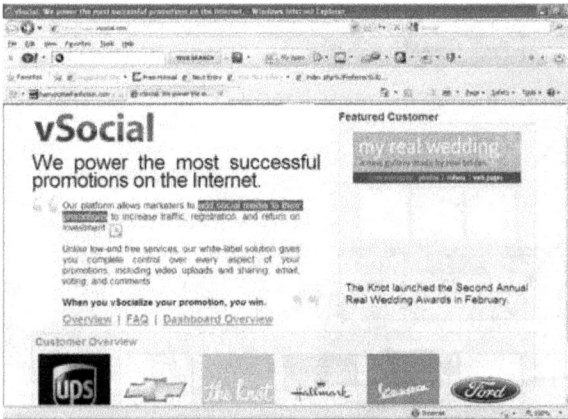

HARO
www.helpareporter.com/about-haro

The website brings reporters, bloggers, new sources and small
businesses together to tell their stories and promote their products
and services. Registration to HARO is currently free.

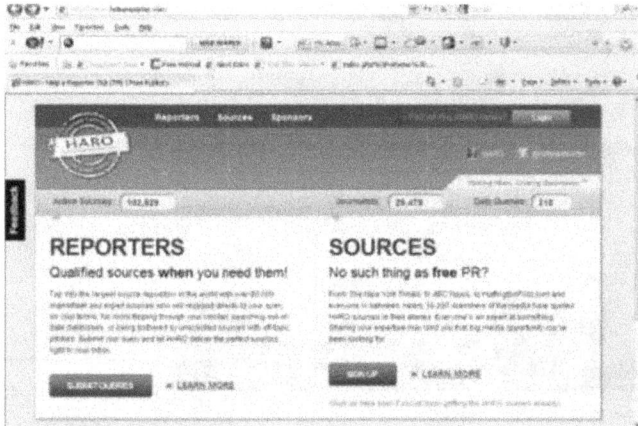

Active Rain,com

This is one of the most popular social networks in the Real Estate
niche.

Doostang.com

This is a pay to use career community that helps elite young professionals accelerate their careers.

Chapter 6

General Networking Sites

General networking sites do not target any particular niche area, but allow users to form their own groups based on their topics of interest. The membership of the more popular General networking sites runs in millions, this means that by joining them you can potentially target a huge market. They also offer search features through which you can look for members according to their age groups, professions, interests and even geographical locations. The following is a list of the best general networking sites on the web, that you can gain leverage from.

Facebook.com

This is one of the most popular social networking websites on the net. It has millions of users and offers its members advanced search features, advertising plans as well as the option to form groups based on their areas of interest. Sign up to Facebook is free.

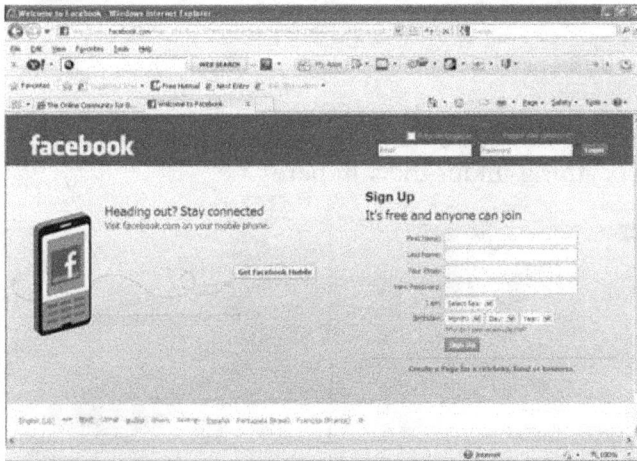

Twitter.com

This has become one of the most popular social networking websites with a regular and loyal user base from round the world. Twitter has a lot of celeberity users as well. Membership to the site is free.

Wikipedia.com

This website hardly needs any introduction. You can share information about everything under the sun here!

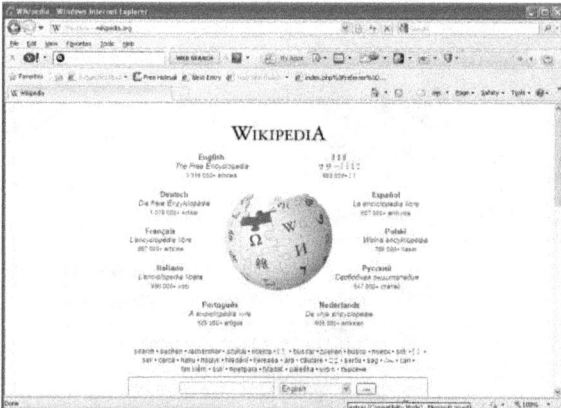

Bebo.com

The social networking site allows members to share their pictures, videos, opinions, blogs, etc, with each other. Sign up to Bebo is free.

43 Things.com

Joining this community can help you network and connect with people who have the same goals and ambitions as you. Membership to 43 Things is free.

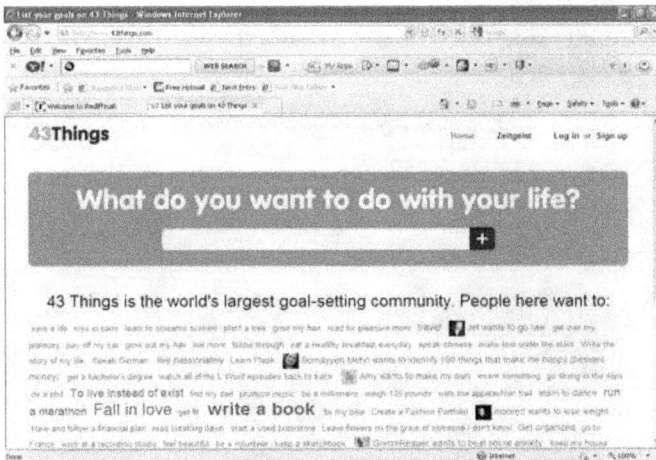

MySpace;com

My space is a popular networking site with millions of members from all across the globe. You can become a member of the network for free.

Yahoo! Answers.com

The website allows users to ask questions about anything under the sun and the community members post answers. The network is a great way to build your brand by answering questions related to your niche area. Membership to Yahoo Answers is free.

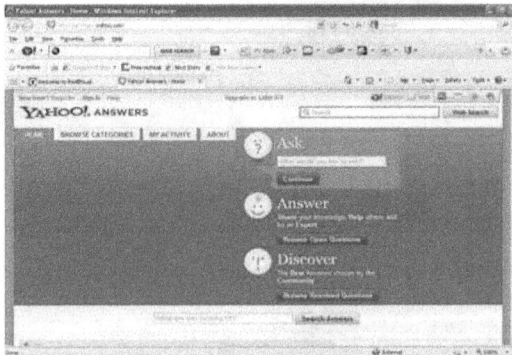

Ning.com

The website allows users to form and join social networks based on their areas of interest. Membership to Ning is free.

Wetpaint.com

The website allows users to build online communities based on their areas of interest. It combines the best features of wikis, blogs and social media websites, i.e. members can post articles, photos, media files, etc, to their online community and express their views on content posted by others. Sign up to Wetapaint is free.

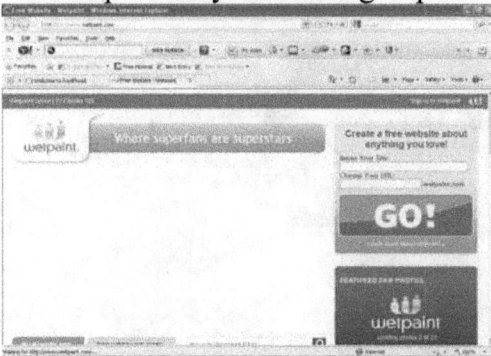

Asmallworld.net

This is a by-invitation only tight knit community of people with similar interests, backgrounds and perspectives.

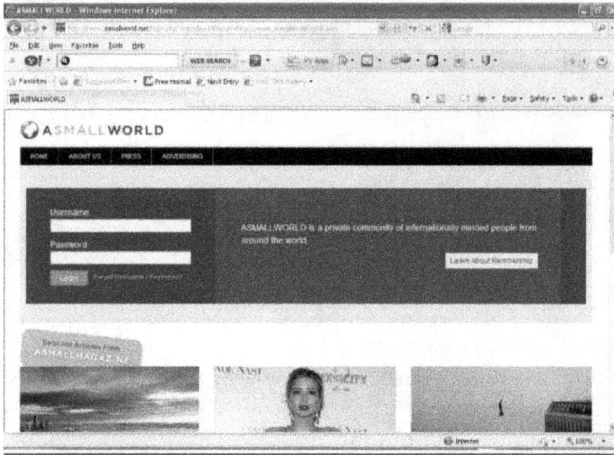

Badoo.com

The social network allows members to meet and interact with people living or working in their area. Membership to the network is free.

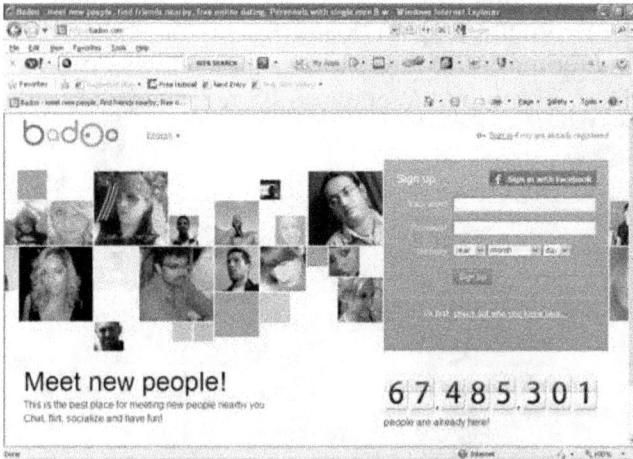

Eons

This is an online community for boomers. Sign up to Eons is free.

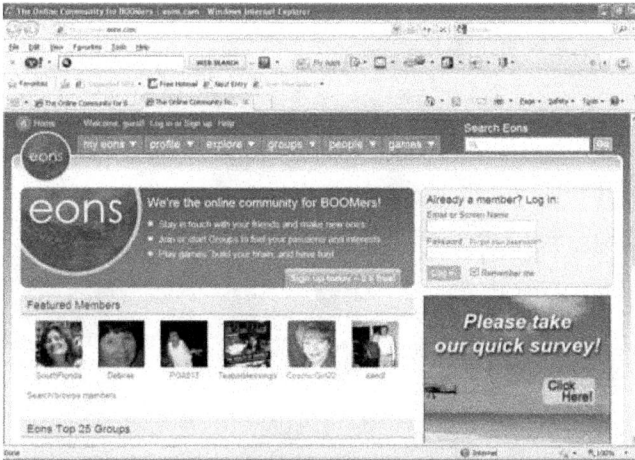

Faceparty.com

Face party is a UK based social networkings site. Sign up to the website is free.

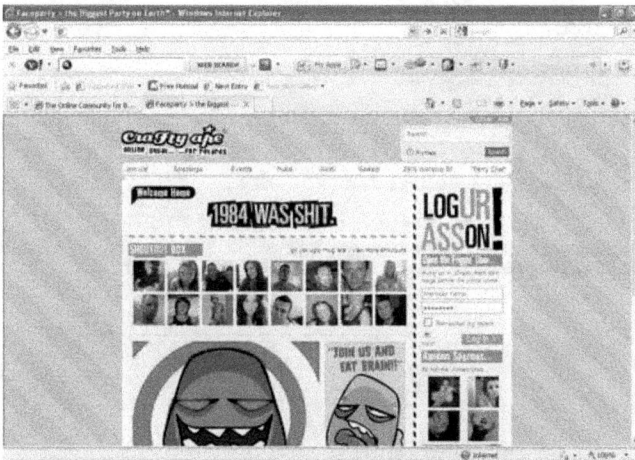

Friendster.com

This is another social networking website with a huge base of active members.

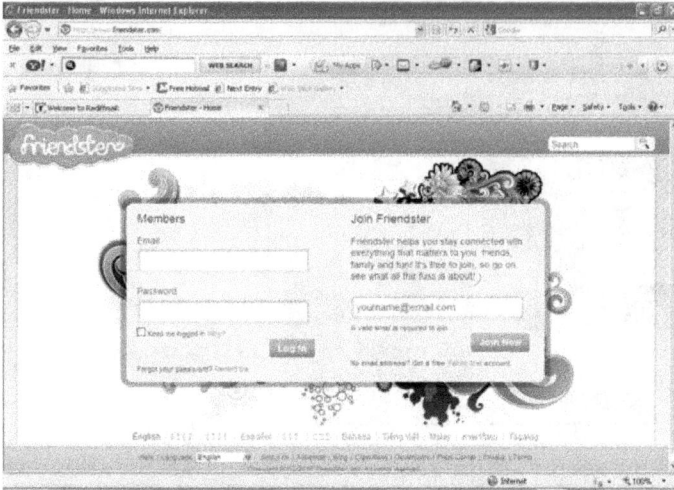

Hi5,com

This social networking community has a large Indian user base. Membership to Hi5 is free.

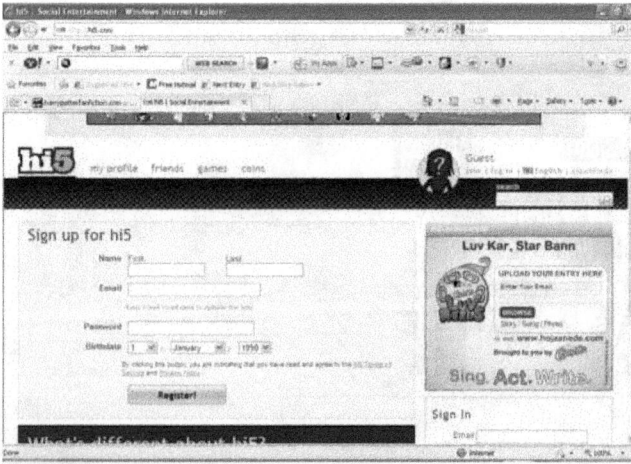

Multiply.com

This family friendly social networking website facilitates sharing of
pictures, blogs, videos, music, reviews, opinions, etc.

Netlog.com

This is a social networking website consisting of more than 6.4
million users from Europe. Sign up to Netlog is free.

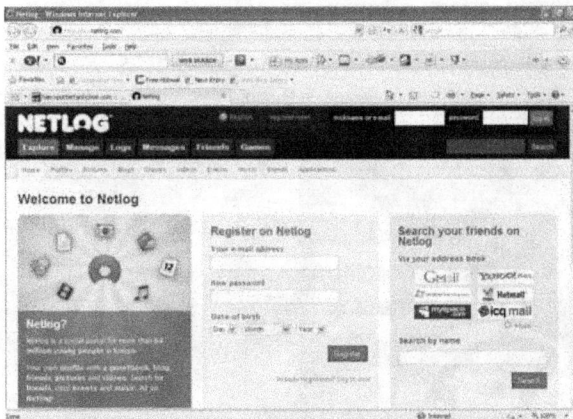

Orkut

www.orkut.co.in

This social networking website is owned by Google and has a huge base of active and loyal users from across the globe.

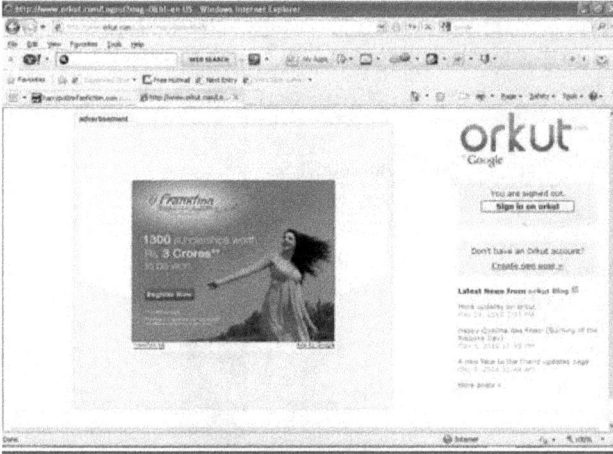

Piczo.com

Piczo is an online community for teenagers. Membership to the website is free.

Plazes.com

This networking site helps users keep those in their network upadatd about their location. It is essentially a service that can help you co-ordinate your real world activities with your contacts. Membership to Plazes is free.

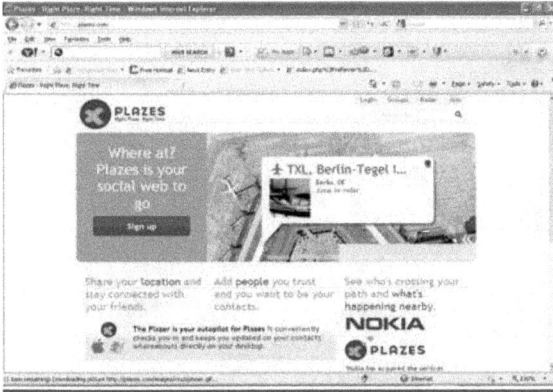

Profileheaven.com

This social network has a huge base of loyal and active users. It actually allows users to create mini sites about themselves. Membership to Profileheaven is free.

Vox.com

This networking website allows users to post their photos, videos, blogs, audio files, etc for free. Vox also offers the added avantage of integrating other networkings services like Youtube and Flickr in one's blog.

Xanga.com

This social networking website allows users to host weblogs, videoblogs, audioblogs as well as photoblogs. You can sign up to Xanga for free, though you may have to pay more for premium services.

Xuqa.com

This is a popular networking website dedicated to gaming. You can sign up to Xuqa for free.

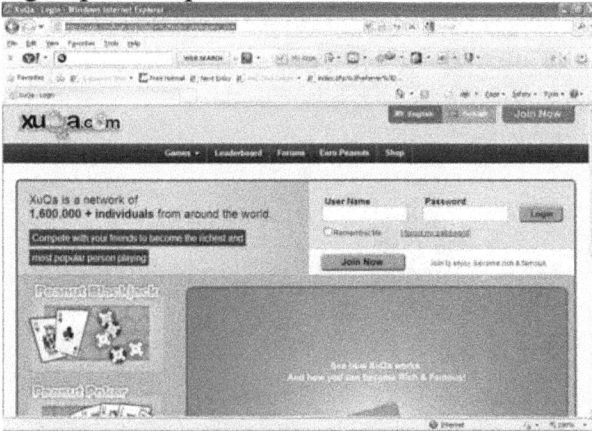

Tagged.com

This social network helps its members make new contacts through features like social games, browsing profiles, group interests, etc. Membership to Tagged is free.

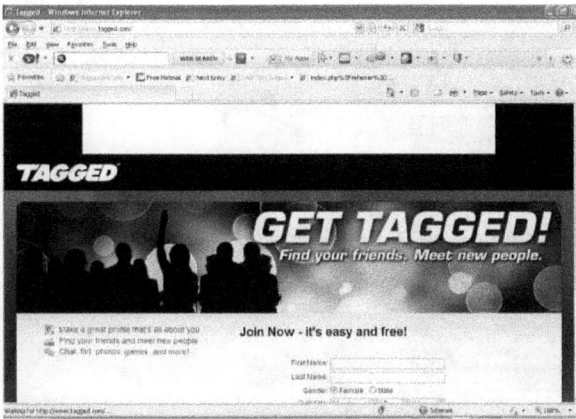

Meetup.com

This website helps people with similar interests form offline clubs or meetup groups in their local area. Meetup has members from some 45,000 cities across the globe. You can sign up for free, but you may have to pay for using premium services.

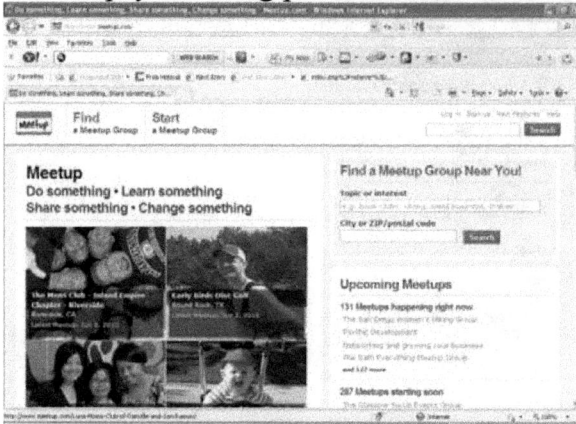

Mylife.com

Mylife is a popular US based people search engine. You can use it to expand your network and stay in touch with your existing contacts, by registering for free.

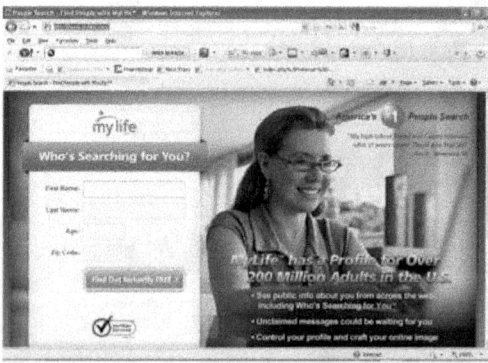

Blackplanet.com

This is a popular social networking website for African Americans. You can sign up to Blackplanet for free.

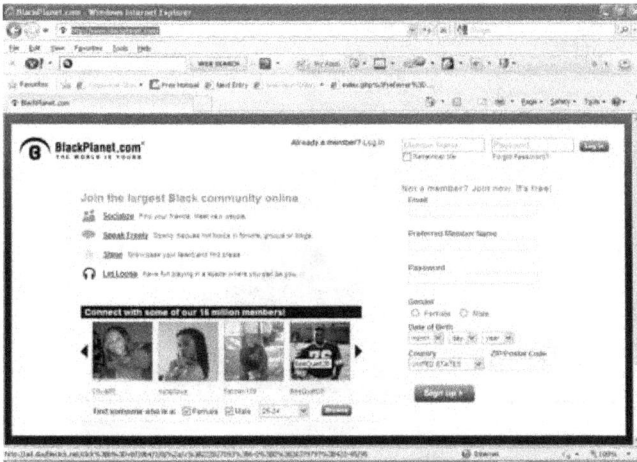

SkyRock.com

The social networking website offers its members free web space where they can create a blog and exchange messages. It also has a special section where members can upload their original music compositions.

Ping.fm

The website allows its users to manage their social networks through a single login. Sign up to Ping.fm is free.

CoRank.com

This is a general information sharing network. Registration to CoRank is free.

CommonGate connects people who share common interests and passions.

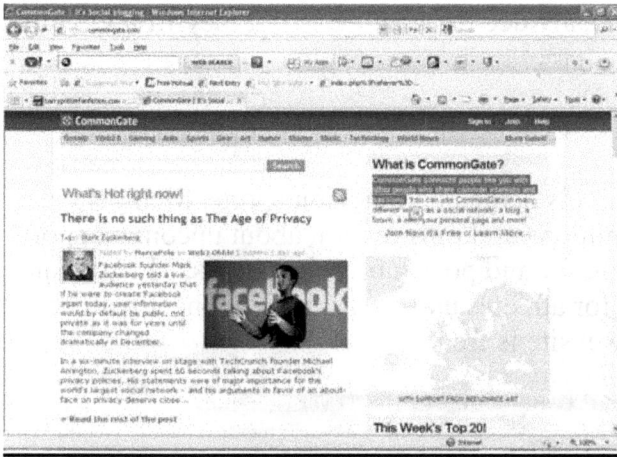

Chapter 7
Niche specific Networking sites

As the name suggests these networking websites are based on certain niche areas. From a marketers point of view these websites are perhaps more important than general social networking websites, because they have a user base with clearly defined tastes and interests. So, you can easily decide whether or not they fit into your target market.

ActionProfiles.com

This networking website is dedicated to action sports. Members can not only share their opinions and information about upcoming sports events but can also look for and post sport related jobs. The website also offers a platform for athletes and sponsors to connect with each other. Sign up to the website is free.

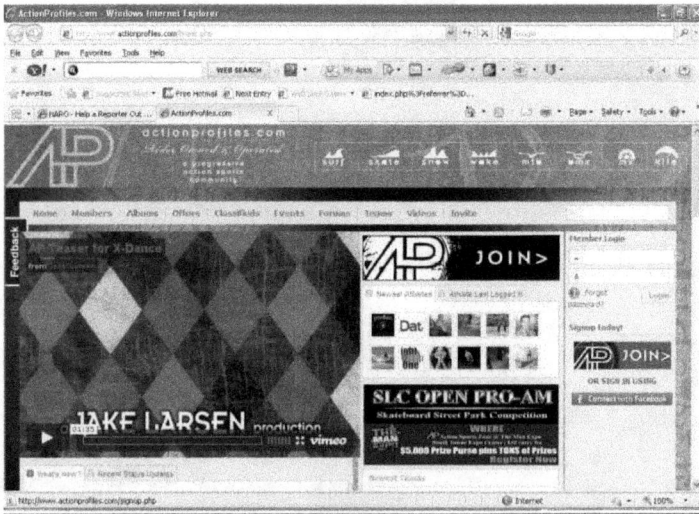

ArtSlant.com

This is a networking community for sharing information and news about artists and art events across the globe. Registration to the site is free.

BeGreen.com

This social network connects people who believe in the 'green living program' and are committd to spreading awarness about it. Registration to the website is free.

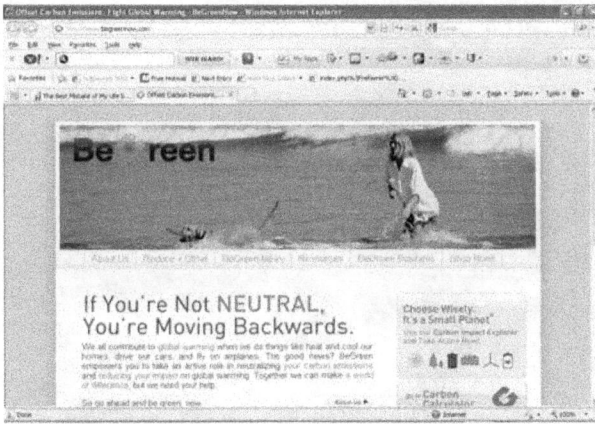

Be Recruited.com

This social networking websites allows high school athletes to connect with college coaches. Registration to Be Recruited is free.

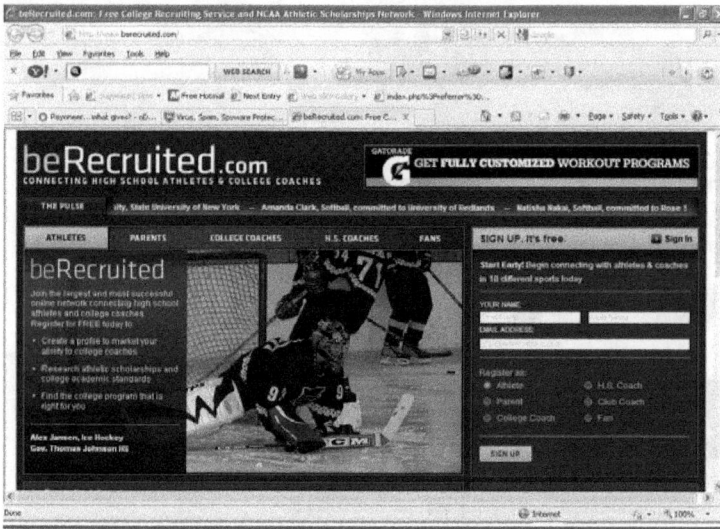

Bottletalk.com

This social networking website is for Wine enthusiasts, it allows users to share their opinions and stories about different kinds of wine.

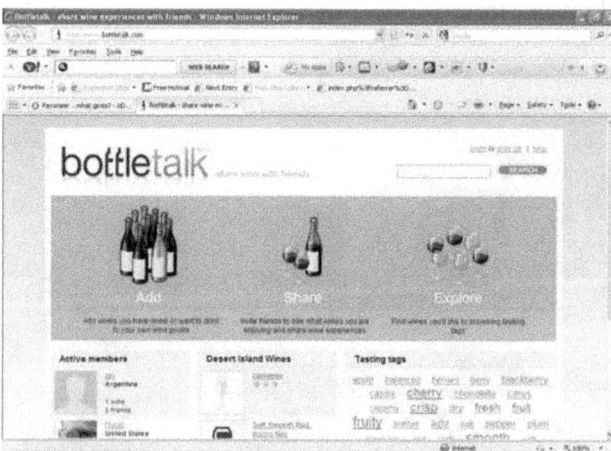

CarGurus.com

This is a networking website for Car lovers. It's a great place to post and read reviews about cars and find the best used car deals. You can sign up to the website for free.

Change.org

This is a networking website for people who believe in a cause and want to make a difference. Registration to the website if free.

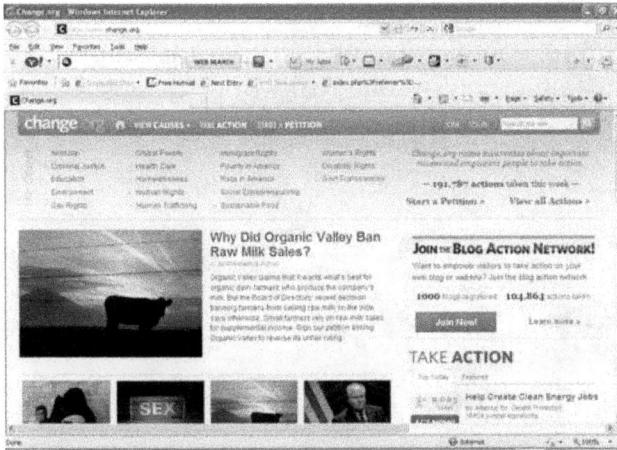

Changing the present.org

This is a network for nonprofit organizations and people who believe in causes. The website offers users a platform to communicate and collaborate so that they can promote their causes and make a difference to the world around them. You can sign up to Changingthepresent for free.

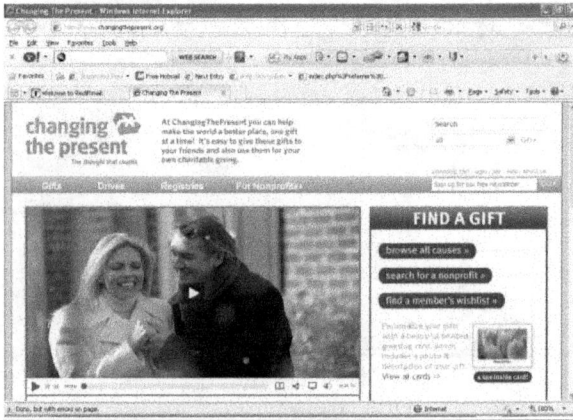

CircleUp.com

The website provides group communications services that allow users to stay in touch with their online and real world contacts. Registration to the website is free.

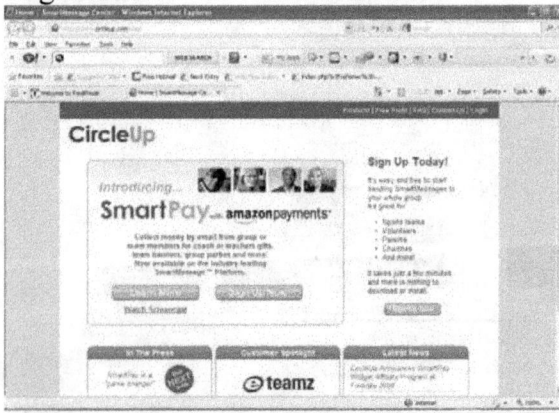

DailyStrength.org

This is a health based social network where users support each other with their health issues and share medical information. You can sign up to the website for free.

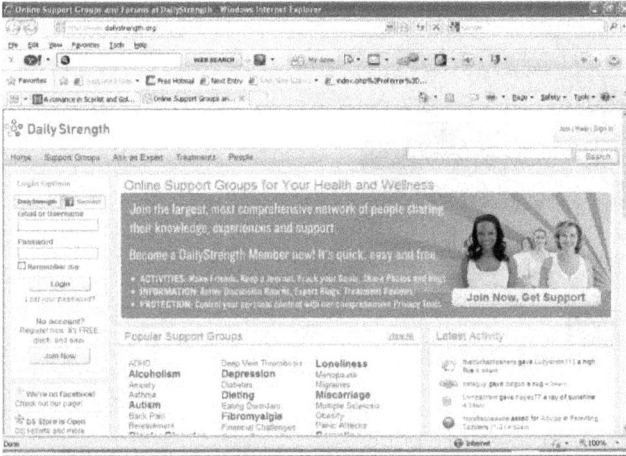

Flixster.com

This is a social network for movie buffs. Users can share information and their opinions/views about any aspect of movies. Membership to Flixster is free.

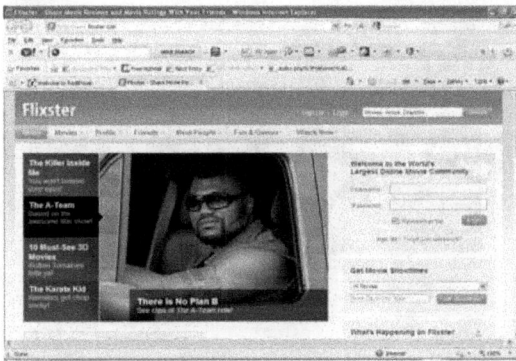

Girlsense.com

This social networking website for fashionistas allows them to share their designs, opinions, news and views about the fashion world. Registration to the website is free.

Greenvoice.com

This social network is dedicated to creating awareness about environmental issues. Sign up to the website is free.

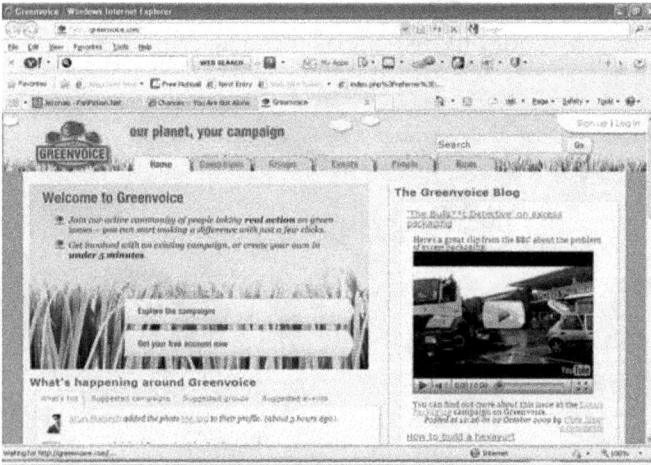

MyCatspace.com

This is an online community for cat lovers. Registration to the website is free.

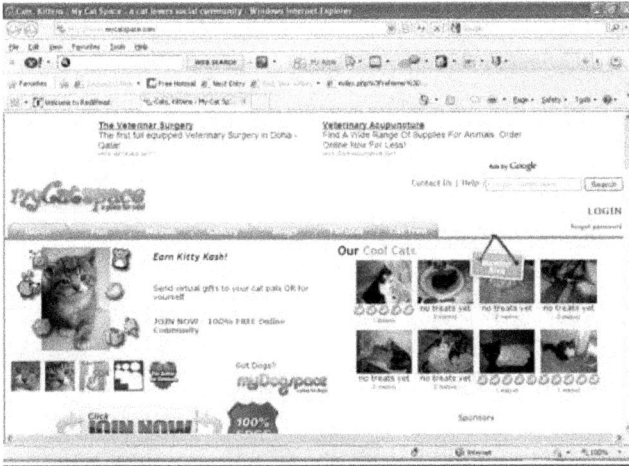

My Dog Space.com

This is an online community for dog lovers. Registration to the website is free.

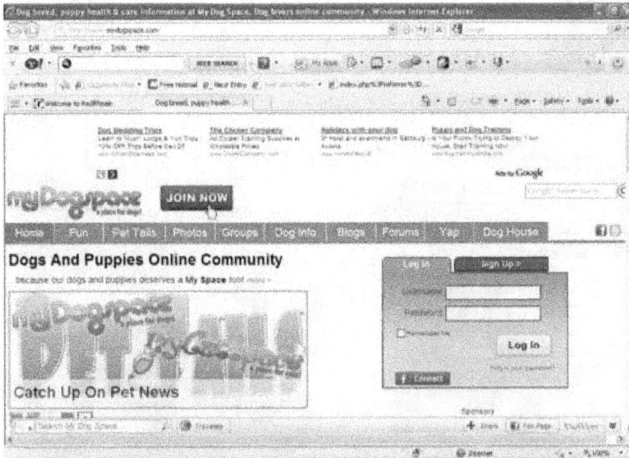

Uniteddogs.com

This is another social networking website for dog lovers.
Registration to Uniteddogs is free.

Chuala.com

This is an interactive pronunciation index that helps users learn to
speak different languages. It provides a platform for language
students and teachers to interact with each other. Registration to
Chuala is free.

Babbel.com

Babbel is a pay for use language learning community that offers its users interactive media applications as well as the facility to interact with other language students and teachers.

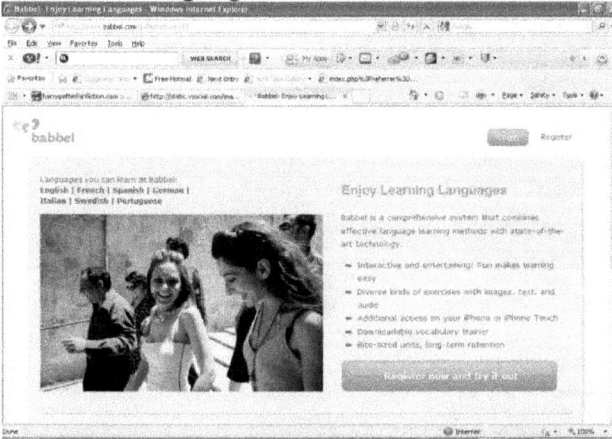

Huitalk.com

Huitalk is another interactive community for people learning new languages. Registration to the website is free.

Italki.com

This is a networking website where you can find partners to practice your language skills. You can join Italk for free. It is a great meeting place for language teachers and students.

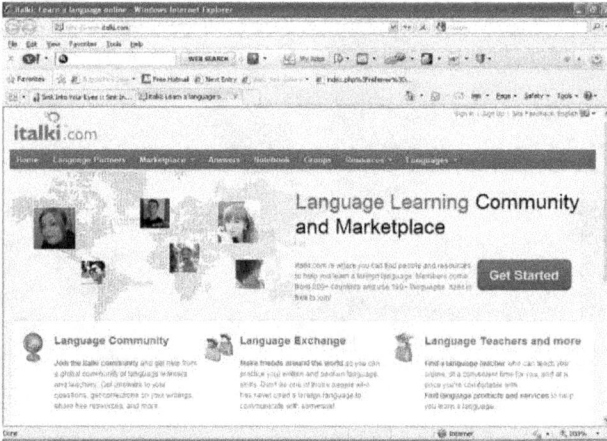

KanTalk.com

This is an interactive community that helps its users learn and practice English. You can join KanTalk for free.

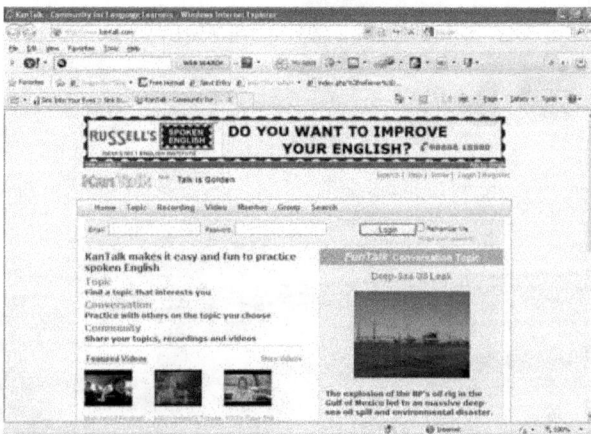

LiveMocha.com

This is another language learning community that allows users to practice their language skills with native speakers and teachers. It also offers a lot of interactive media applications. You can join Livemocha for free but you will have to pay for enrolling in online courses.

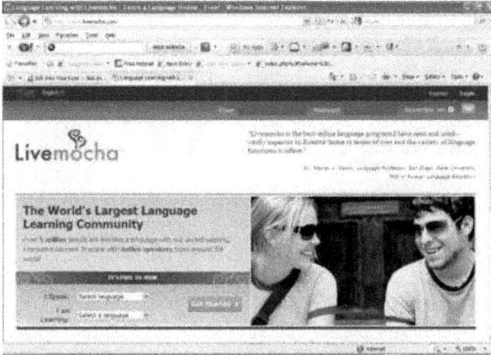

My Language Exchange.com

The site helps connect users who are learning each other's language, so that they can practice their language skills by conversing with a native speaker. Joining the website is free, but you will have to pay for using premium services.

Novlet.com

This networking website for amateur and aspiring writers supports collaborative non-linear story writing in different languages. You can sign up to the website for free.

OLAC
www.language-archives.org

The website is dedicated to creating a virtual library of language resources. You can join the OLAC's mailing list for free.

Shared Talk.com

This is a language exchange and learning community with a huge user base. You can join the online community for free.

Talkbean.com

This is a great networking site for language teachers as they can get paid to take online lessons. Registration to the website is free.

Talk Conmigo.com

This is Barcelona's most popular language exchange community as well as an online guide to local events and gigs. Registration to the website is free.

TopLanguageCommunity.com

This is a community of multi-lingual and bi-lingual people living in UK and Ireland. Through this website you can find language teaching jobs, dates, flat-mates, information about local events and gigs, etc. Registration to the Top Language Community is free.

Unilang.org

This is another networking website that allows its users to practice and learn new languages. You can join the Unilang community for free.

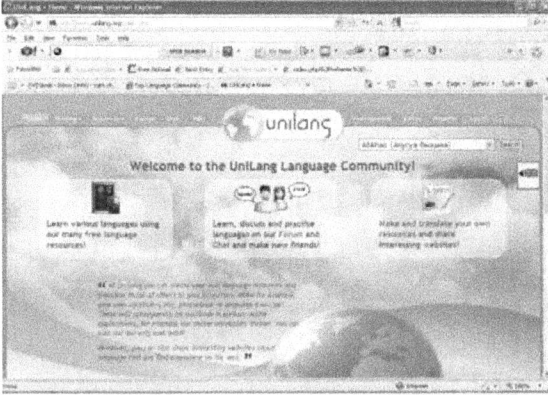

Footnote.com

This pay to use social networking website is dedicated to history buffs. It allows users to share and find rare historical documents.

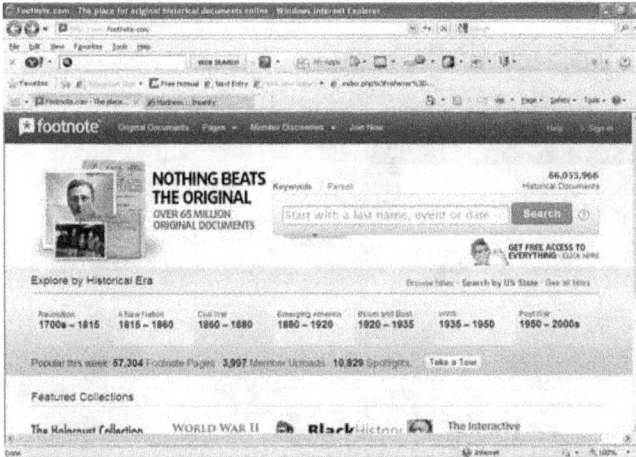

Birdpost.com

This social networking website for bird-watching enthusiasts allows them to share their bird sightings experiences and access information about birds by region, name or physical characteristics. Sign up to Birdpost is currently free.

Coastr.com
This is a free social networking website for Beer lovers.

Gaiaonline.com

This is a popular and award winning social gaming and networking website. You can sign up to the website for free.

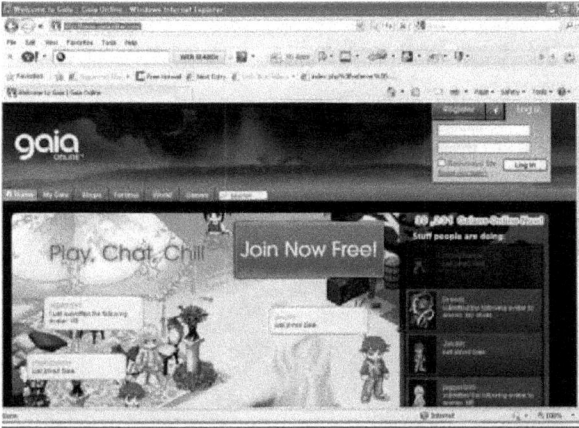

Comicspace.com

This is social networking website of comic lovers. It currently has over 44,000 comic book fans and creators as members. You can also buy and sell you comic artworks here. Registration to the website is currently free; however you have to buy primo membership if you want to avail services like selling your artwork.

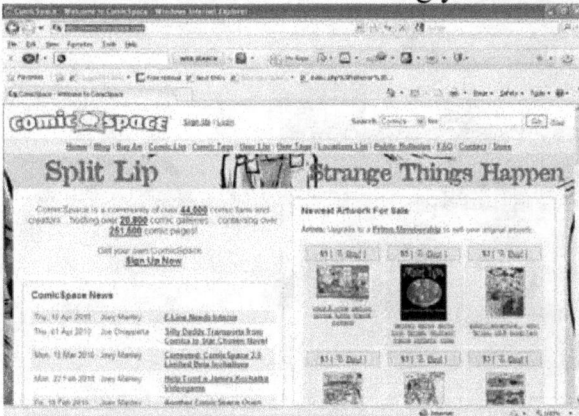

DeviantArt.com

This is a free social networking website for art lovers and artists. It allows its users to track their favorite artists as well buy and sell artwork.

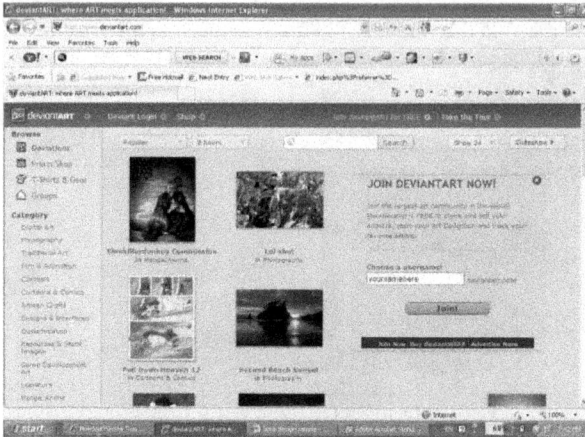

Dogster.com

This is an award winning social networking website for dog owners and lovers. Registration is currently free.

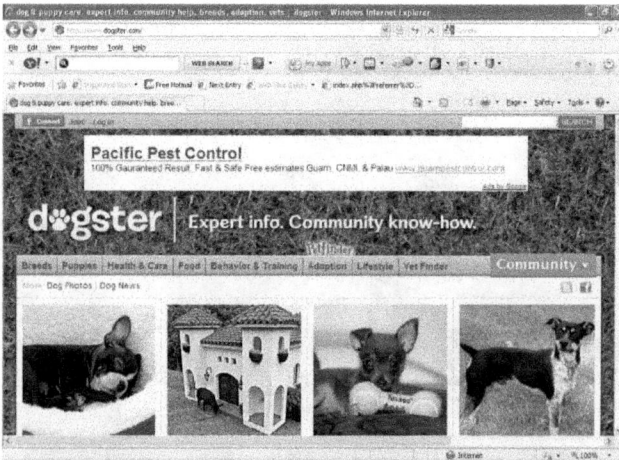

Catster.com

This is an award winning social networking website for cat owners and lovers. Registration is currently free.

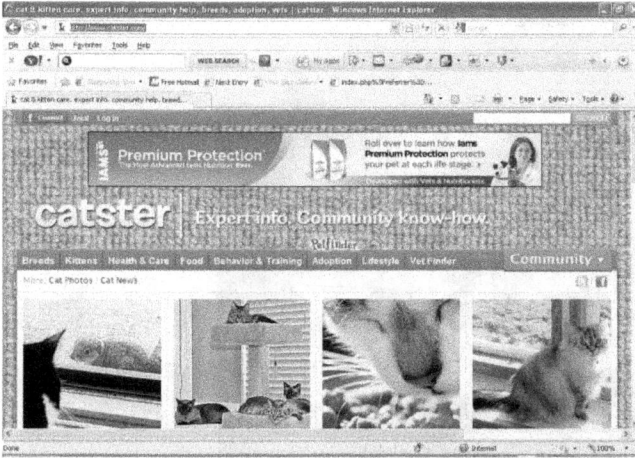

NewGrounds.com

This is a networking website dedicated to gaming. It allows users to upload their home made Flash games and movies and critique those posted by others. You can sign up to the website for free.

Asoboo.com

This is a network of internationally minded creative people.
Registration is currently free.

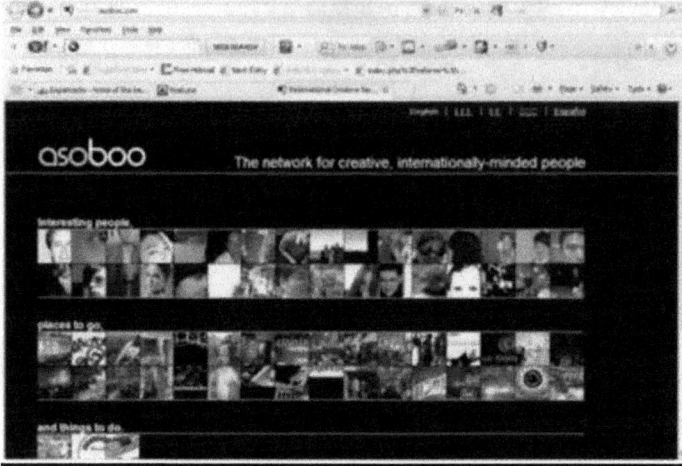

Chapter 8
Video Sharing Hosting and Networking Websites

Youtube really isn't the only video sharing website out there on the web! There are several other platforms where the competition is less intense but the visibility is still high. What's more some of these websites also offer editing tools that can make your videos look more professional.

The biggest advantage of joining video sharing websites is that they can get you noticed faster and if your video is good, you can even earn money from it!
I have also listed a few additional video services websites in this section that you can use to distribute and market your videos.

So, what are you waiting for? Start reading and pick out the video sharing sites that you feel will work best for your business.

You Tube.com
You Tube doesn't need any introduction! It is the 'Big Daddy' of video sharing sites on the internet.

Blip.tv

The site allows users to make independent serialized webshows. The service is free to use currently, however, the website dose have some pay to use features as well.

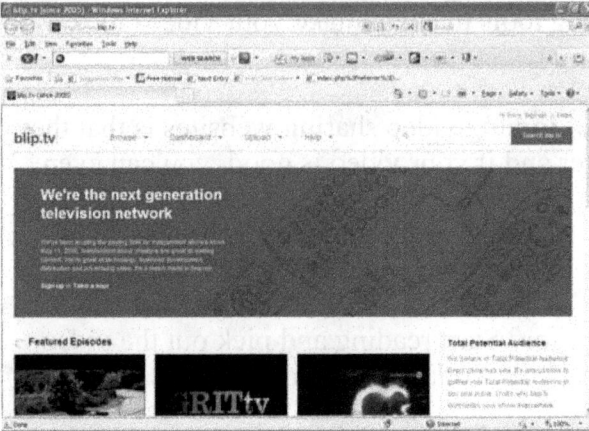

Our Media.com

The website allows users to post and share videos about the causes they support. Registration to the website is currently free.

Veoh.com

This is a popular video content sharing and internet television website. Registration to Veoh is currently free.

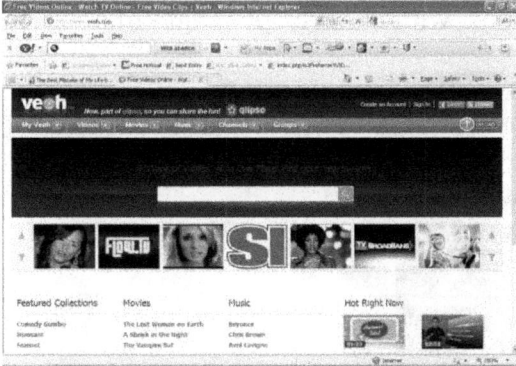

Daily motion.com

This is another video sharing website that allows users to upload their own videos and subscribe to and comment upon other members' video posts. Membership to the website is currently free.

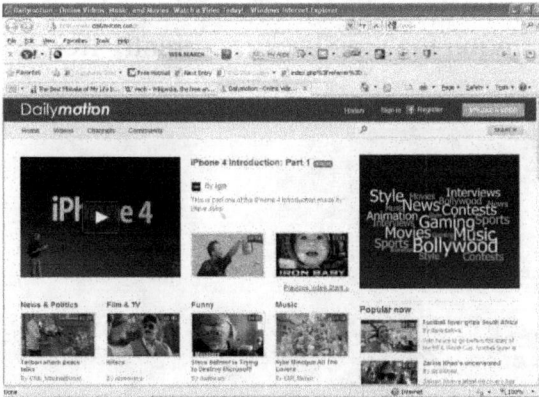

Metacafe.com

This is a popular video entertainment website, where in the community members rank videos. The top ranked ones obviously get maximum visibility. Registration to Metacafe is currently free. Metacafe only hosts short videos, with the average length of a video on the site being 90 seconds.

Clip Shack.com

This is a video sharing website that allows users to post videos/ video blogs, share their clips with friends and family, comment on each other's videos and gain relevant industry information related to digital video creation. Registration to Clip Shack is currently free.

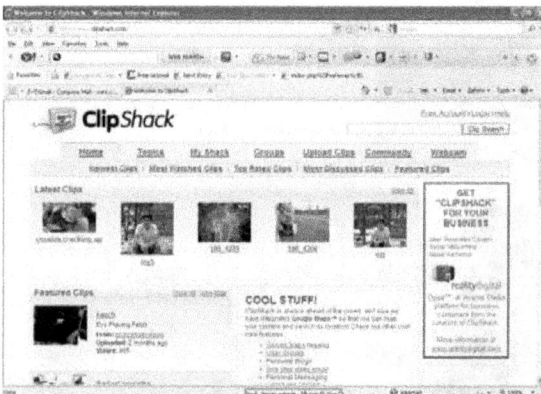

5min.com

This is a Do-it-yourself, video sharing websites. As the name suggest the videos uploaded on the website demonstrate how to do something in 5 minutes. Membership to the website is currently free.

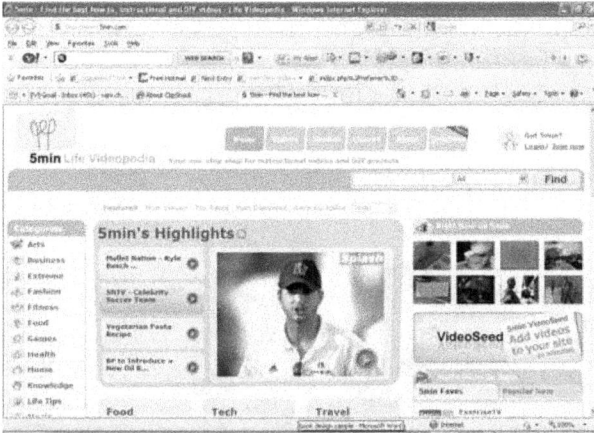

Brightcove.com

This is a pay to use online service that you can use to host, publish and distribute videos to sites on the Web.

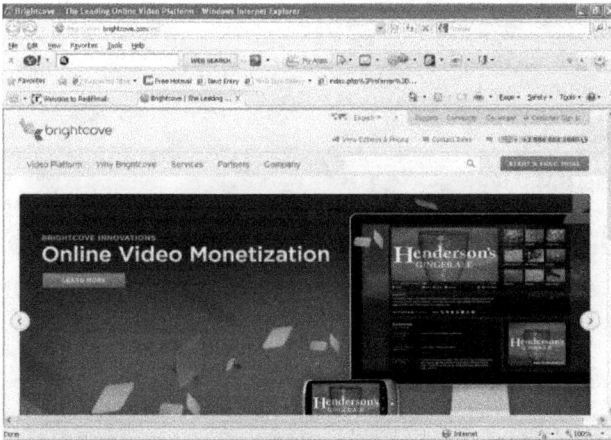

Viddler.com

The video sharing website allows users to record their videos, upload them and comment on others' posts. To use the website for business purposes you need to become a paid member.

Revver.com

This viral video network allows internet marketers to make money from their videos. The website is currently free to use.

Vimeo.com

This is a website that allows its members to create and share their creative videos and short films. The site offers two types of memberships, the basic one is free but users have to pay to use premium services.

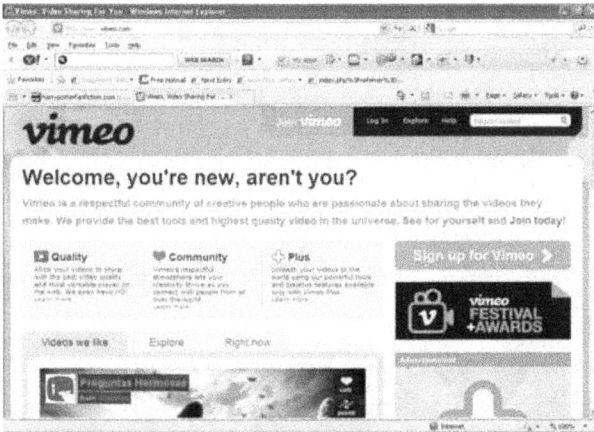

Yahoo Video
www.screen.yahoo.com

As the name suggests it is Yahoo's video sharing website, it features both-user created content and exclusive web shows. Sign up to the website is currently free.

HelpfulVideo.com

The website allows users to publish, buy and sell videos. If your video contains advertising or promotion of a product or service you have to pay to use the website.

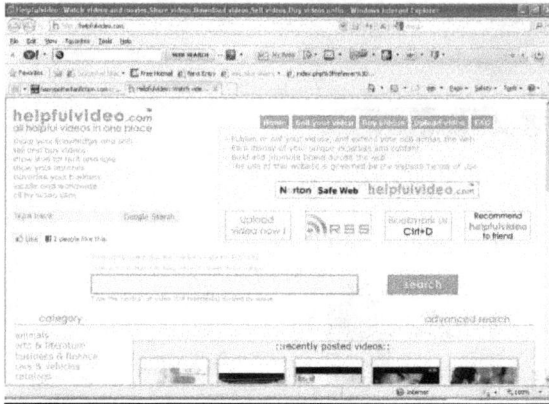

Broadband Sports.com

The site allows users to post and share their sports related videos. Sign up to the website is currently free.

Travelistic .com

The website allows users to post and share their travel videos. The website is currently free to use.

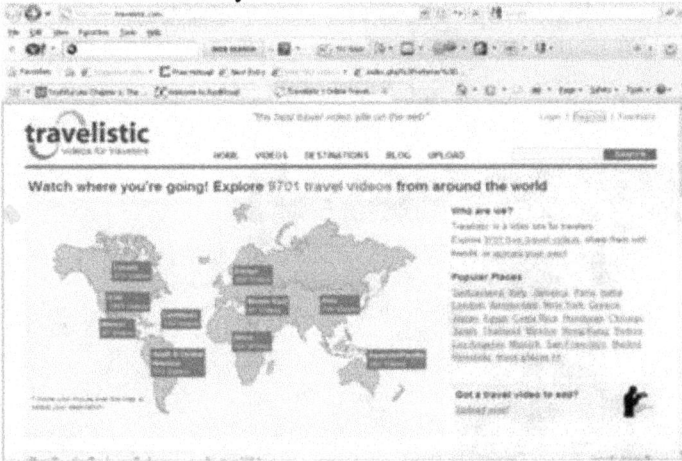

Live Video.com

The site allows users to share their videos and create their own channels. Registration to the website is currently free.

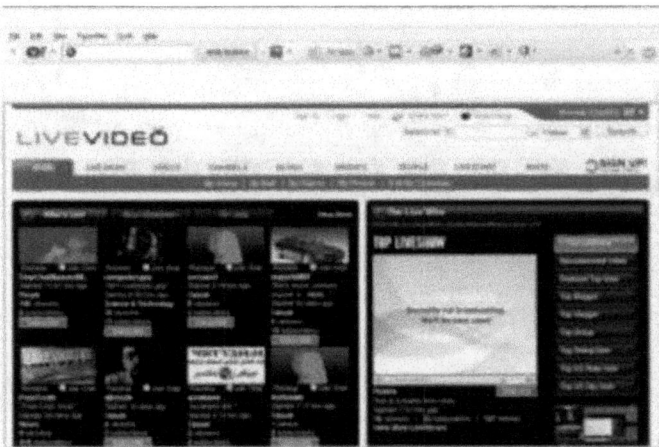

Meet the boss
www.meettheboss.tv

This website offers exclusive video and audio lessons from the world's most innovative and influential business leaders.

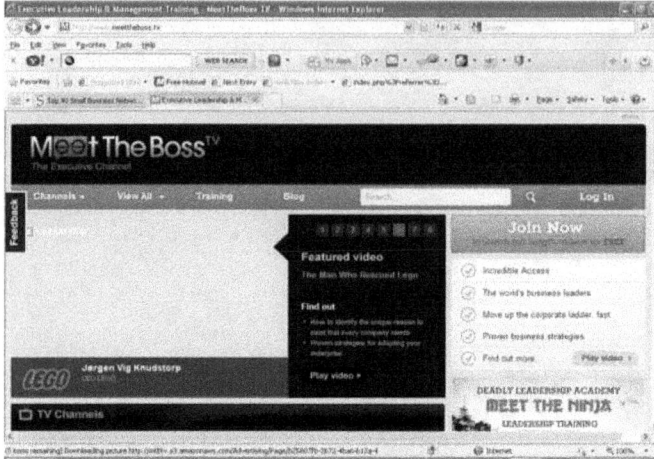

Kewgo.com

This is a European website that offers pay to use video broadcasting services.

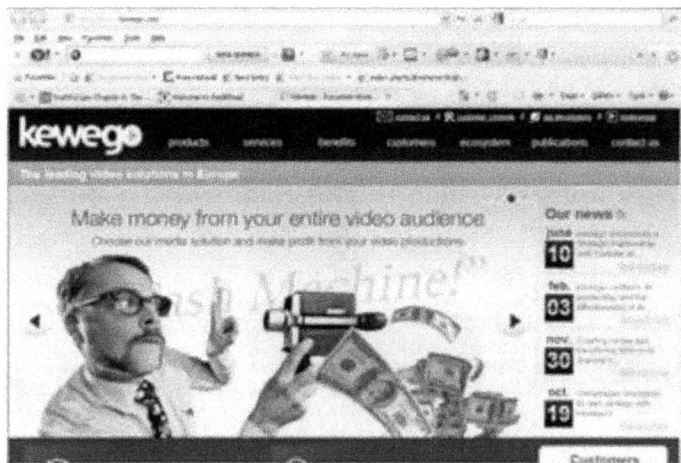

GodTube.com

This is a website for posting and sharing Christian videos. The
website is currently free to use.

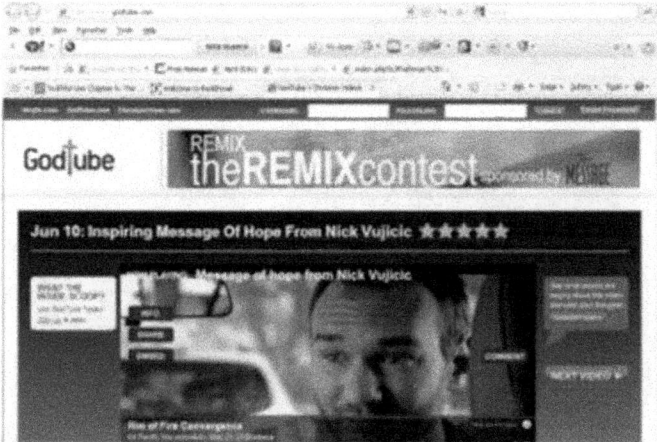

Vmix.com

This is a pay to use media management platform that allows users to
build their brand value and explore new revenue opportunities.

Crackle.com

The video sharing website allows users to upload full length movies, tv shows and other videos. Sign up to the Crackle is currently free.

Break.com

The website allows users to post and share funny videos. Membership to the website is currently free.

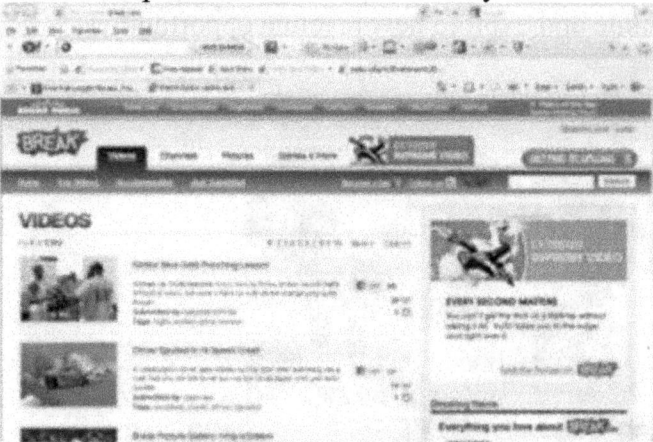

Video Sift.com

The website allows members to post and rate videos. The top rated ones get the maximum visibility.

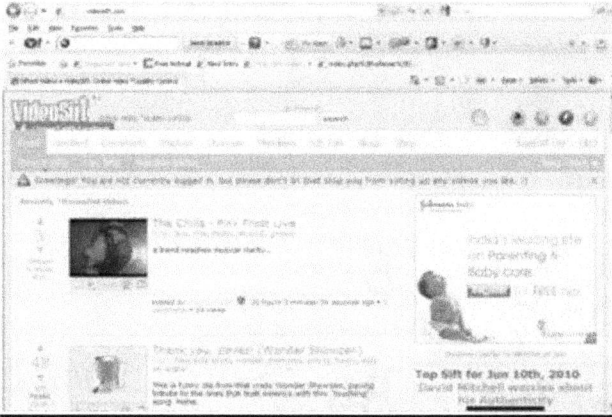

GotGame.com

This is a vidoe sharing website for gaming enthusiasts, where they can uplaod videos related to their favorite game. Sign up to Got Game is currently free.

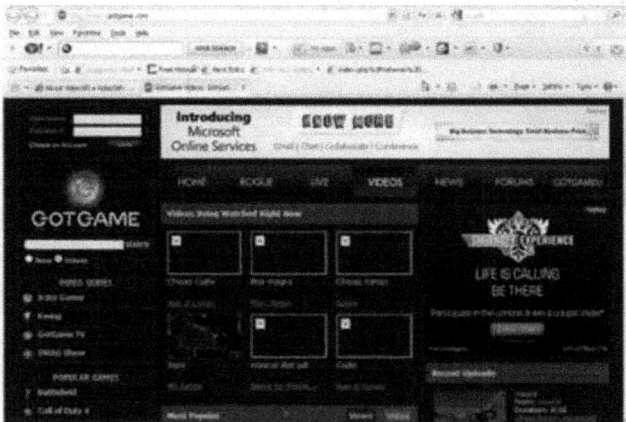

Video Egg.com

Video Egg is a pay to use service that makes it easy for users to upload their videos and post them on multiple video sharing websites.

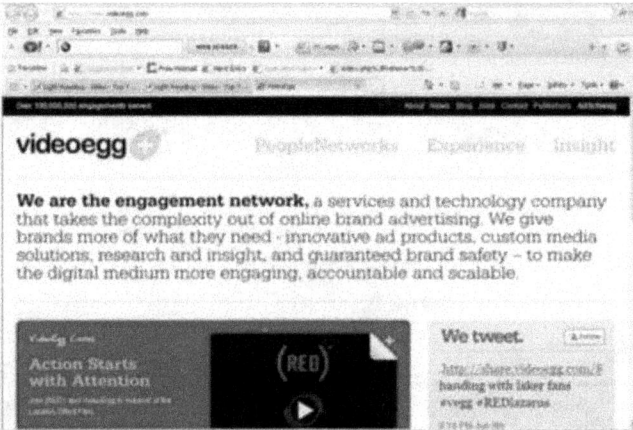

AOL Videos www.on.aol.com

The website allows users to watch exclusive web content and share their videos. It owes its popularity largely to the brand name AOL. Membership to the website is currently free.

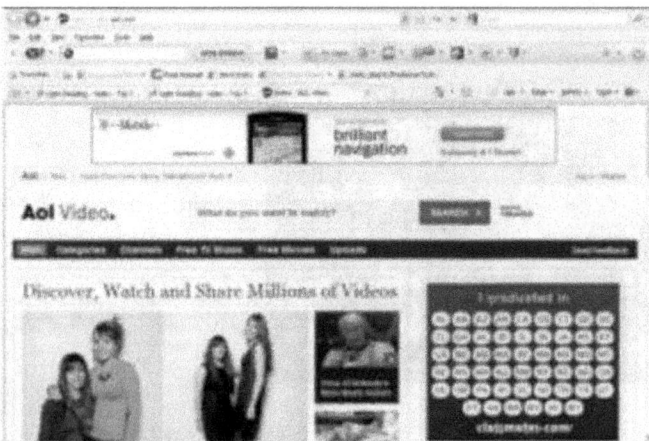

YFrog.com

YFrog allows users to share their pictures and videos on twitter. Membership to the website is currently free.

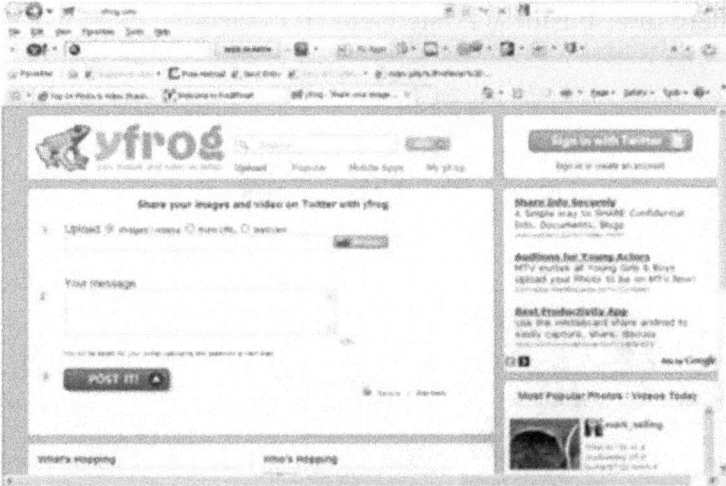

Spike.com

Spike allows users to upload short videos as well as full length films. It also hosts several exclusive web shows. Registration to Spike is currently free.

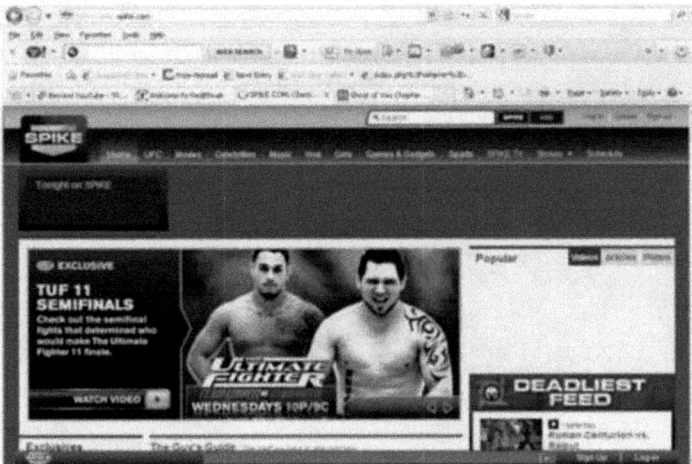

Motion Box.com

This is a video sharing and storage website. Users can sign up and share up to 300 MB personals video for free but have to pay to upload and share their business related and HD videos.

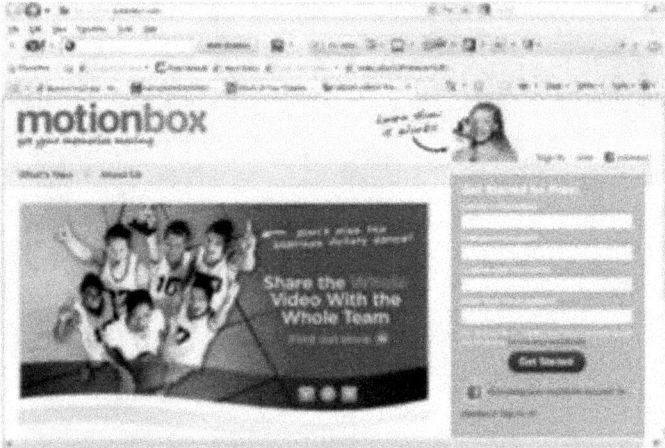

Chapter 9
Live Audio/ Video Steaming

Live audio and video streaming has tremendous potential. These websites can be especially useful for those in the entertainment and consultancy business. You can use live video streaming websites to hold webinars, web-talks and even online coaching sessions. Teleconferencing websites can help consultants take their practice to a global level.
The possibilities are truly endless!

Stickam.com

This is a social networking and video sharing website clubbed into one. Users can make new contacts, hold video chats and even broadcast themselves live. Registration to the website is currently free.

Blog Tv.com

The website allows users to host and produce their own live web based shows. Sign up to the website is currently free.

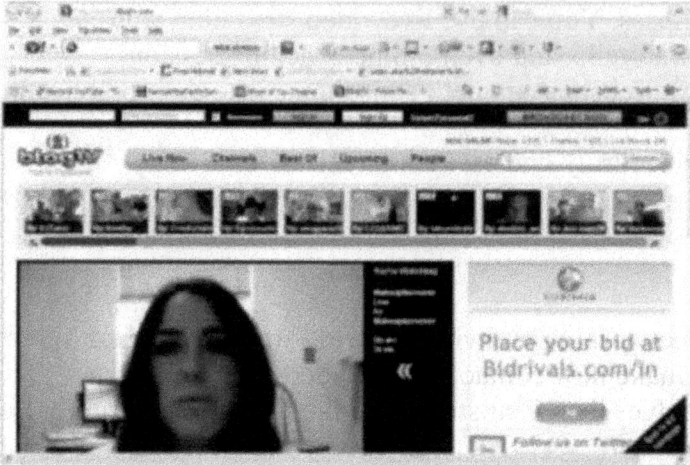

Ovoo.com

The website offers live video chatting and conferencing facility. While the two way video chats are free, users have to pay for holding chats with large groups.

Live Stream.com

The website allows users to start their own live channels and offers several powerful tools to add graphics and effects to videos. Live Stream offers both free as well as premium memberships.

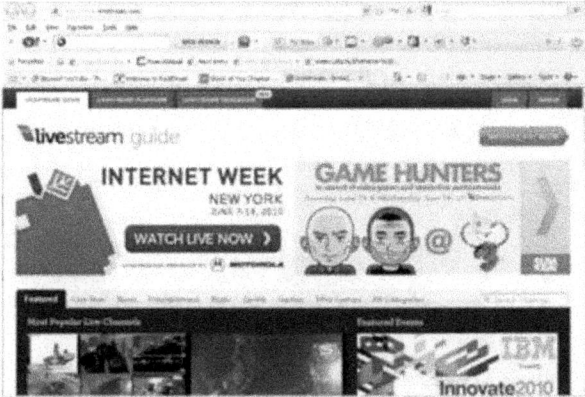

UStream.com

The website allows users to broadcast live videos and offers several powerful tools to make them look professional. Sign up is free; however, you may have to pay for some additional services.

Free Conferencing
www.freeconferencecall.com

The website allows users to make upto 6 hour long free confenece
calls with a maximum number of 96 callers connected at one time.
Participants have to pay their carriers for long distance calls

Chapter 10
Image Hosting and Sharing Websites

A picture truly is worth a thousand words! A great picture can help you attract more traffic than a lengthy well written article. No matter what business you are in, image sharing websites can help you showcase you best wares!

For photographers and artists picture sharing websites can bring in a lot of business. Others can use them as a platform to advertise their products covertly.

There are several niche photo sharing websites on the web as well. You should therefore browse through this list carefully and identify those websites that are likely to have a user base that is most likely to fit into your target market/potential clientele.

Flickr.com

Flickr hardly needs any introduction, it is the Big Boy among the photo sharing websites. You can sign up to Flickr for free.

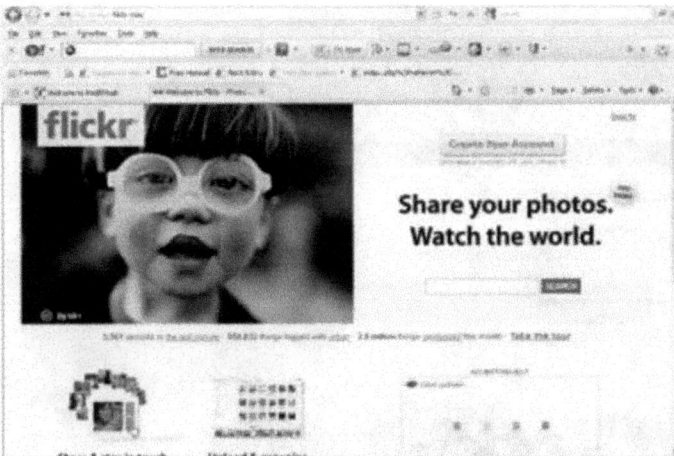

Picasa,com

Picasa is Google's photo sharing and storage website. You can sign in to Picasa with you Google account.

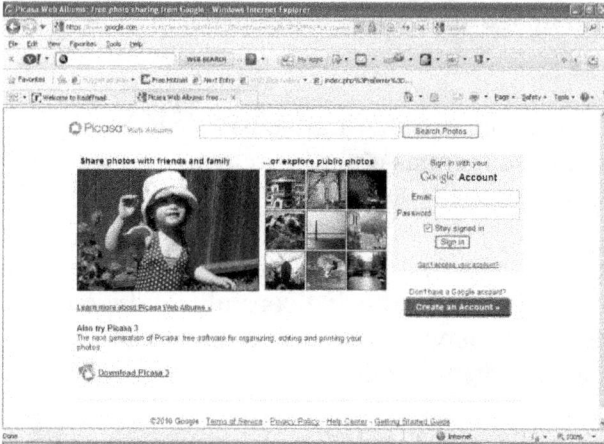

Photo Bucket.com

This is one of the most popular online photo sharing websites. Photobucket is currently free to use.

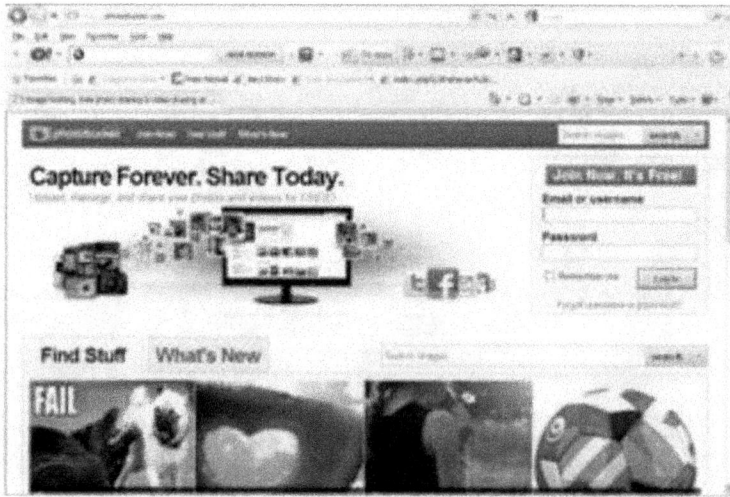

Webshots.com

This website has one of the largest photo libraries on the internet. You can buy and sell your prints on Webshots. The website offers two types of memberships- Free and Premium.

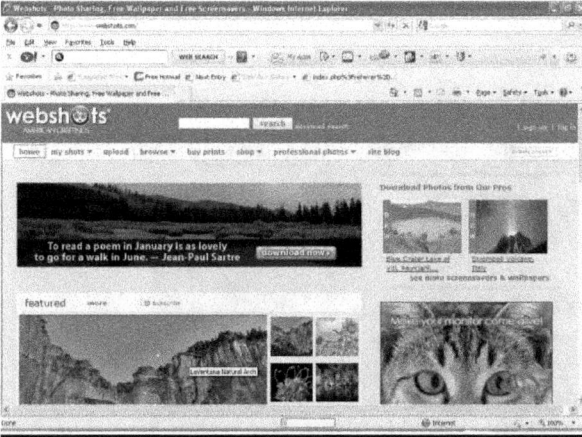

Zorpia
www.in.zorpia.com

This is a social networking website that allows user to share their pictures. Sign up is currently free; however, premium services are chargeable.

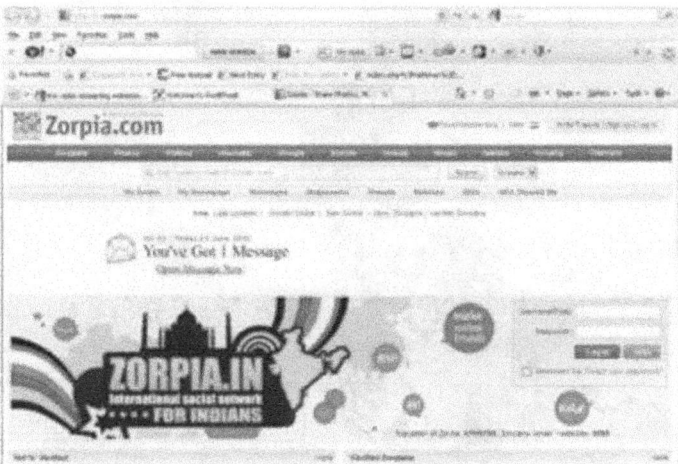

SnapPages.com

This networking website not only allows users to upload and share their photos but also helps them create and edit their own web pages. Personal membership is free, professional and developer memberships, however, are chargeable.

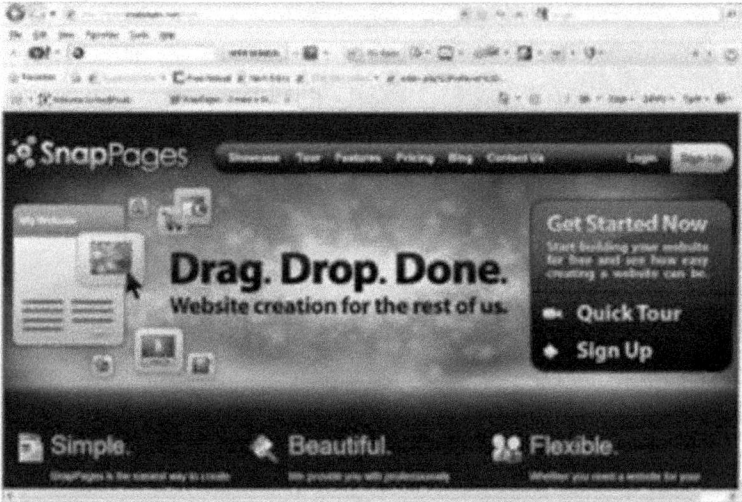

SlideShare.com

This website allows users to share their PowerPoint Presentations, Documents (Word and PDF) and hold webinars. Registration to SlideShare is currently free.

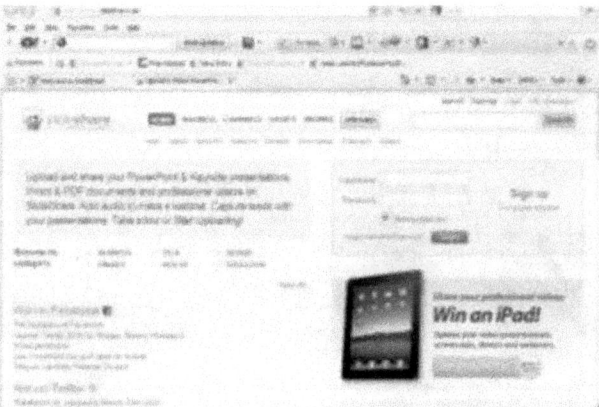

Zoom And Go.com

The website allows users to share their travel related pictures. Registration to the website is currently free.

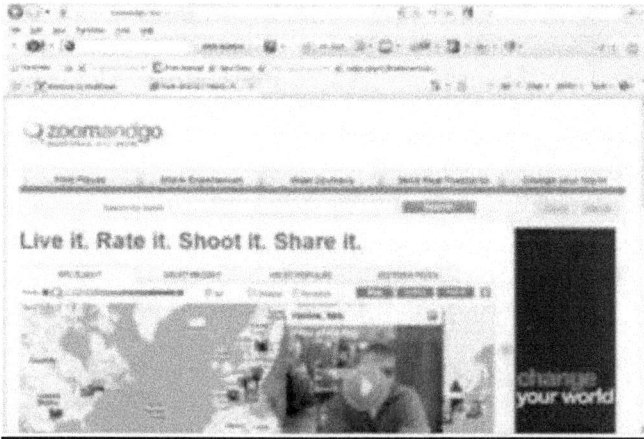

DPhoto.com

This is a powerful photo sharing and storage website. DPhoto offers free trials, but if you want to become a member you have to choose from one of the three pay to use options on the site.

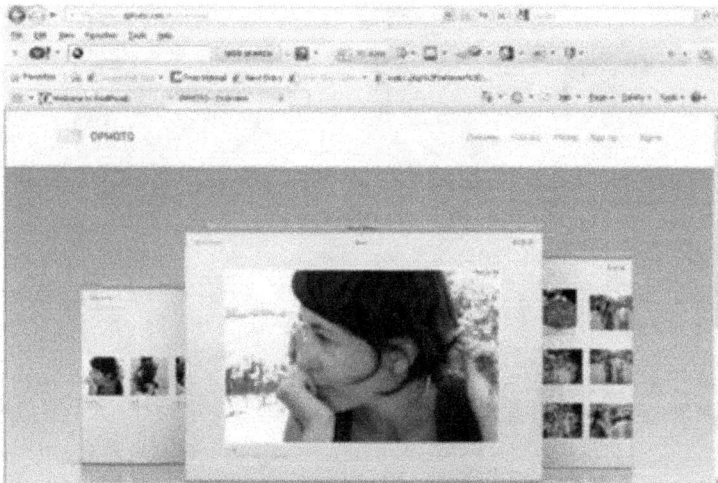

Contakme.com

This is a great photo sharing and networking website for artists, creative professionals, photographers and even writers and musicians. You can create an account on the website for free.

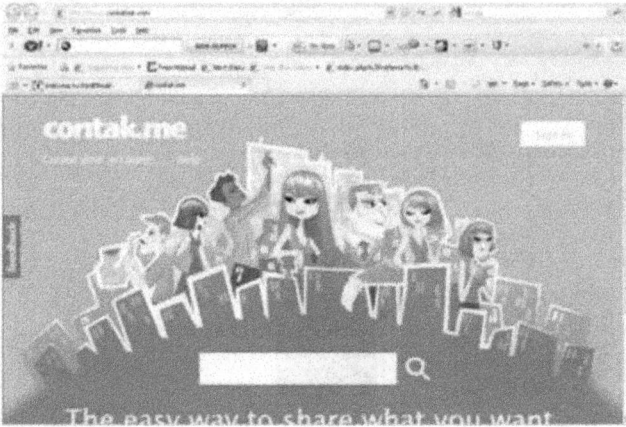

Care2connect.com

This is a unique photo sharing website that allows users to share their pictures and connect with like minded people who believe in making a difference to the world. You can join Care2connect for free.

DotPhoto.com

The site allows users to share their photos, create slideshows with music and narration and also offers print buying and selling services. You can join the website for free, but have to pay for using premium services.

SendPhotos.com

This is a popular online photo sharing website that also offers unique cell phone integration services. You can join SendPhotos for free.

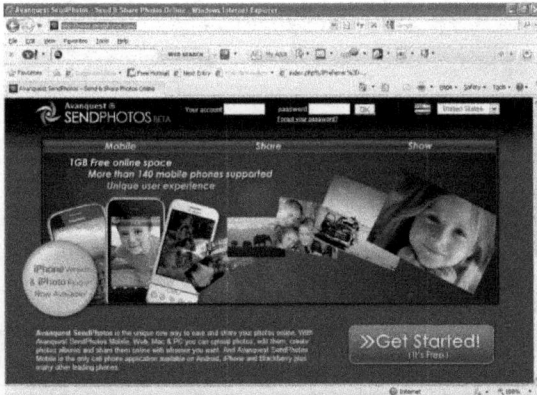

Smugmug.com

This pay to use website offers easy to use photo uploading and sharing tools. It's a spam and ad free website and offers a free 7 day trial.

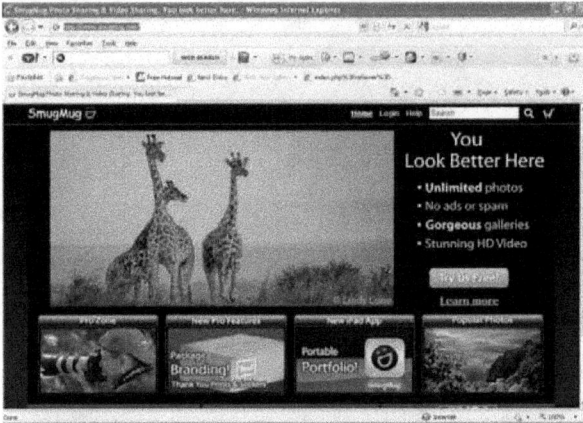

KodakEasyShare.com

This is another photo sharing website that offers easy to use tools to upload and share your pictures. You can also buy prints and photo related gifts on the website. You can join KodakEasyShare for free.

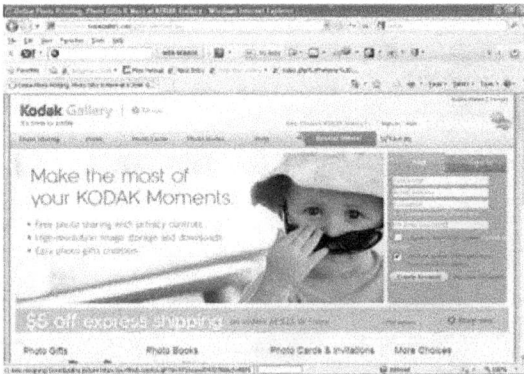

Chapter 11
Music Based Networking Websites

Whether you are an artist, band owner, venue manager/owner or work in the music industry in any capacity, music based networking websites can provide you a lot of exposure.

Most music based networking sites on the web allow artists to upload their music for free. This provides a great opportunity for new and aspiring musicians to get noticed. These websites in fact also provide an excellent platform for people in the music industry to network and connect with each other.

Ilike **.com**

The networking website allows users to share music recommendations, news/information related to concerts as well as their playlists with each other. You can sign up to Ilike for free.

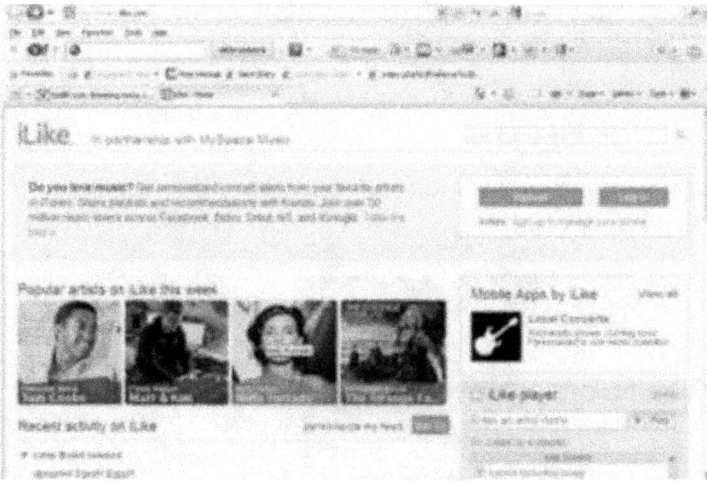

PureVolume.com

The website is dedicated to sharing music. Registration for both listeners and artists is free; however, you have to pay for using premium services.

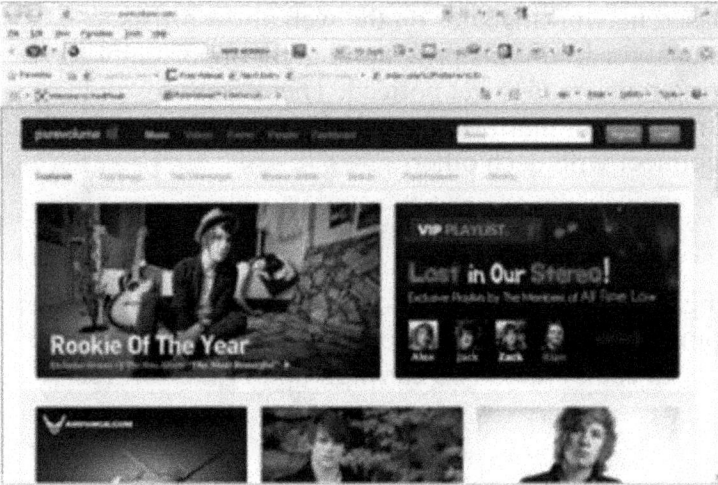

Playlist.com

The website allows you to create free playlists and share them on your favorite social networks.

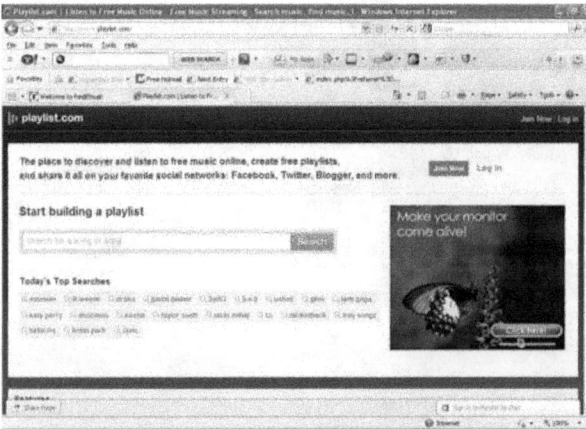

Mp3.com

This is an artist based social network. Sign up to Mp3 is free.

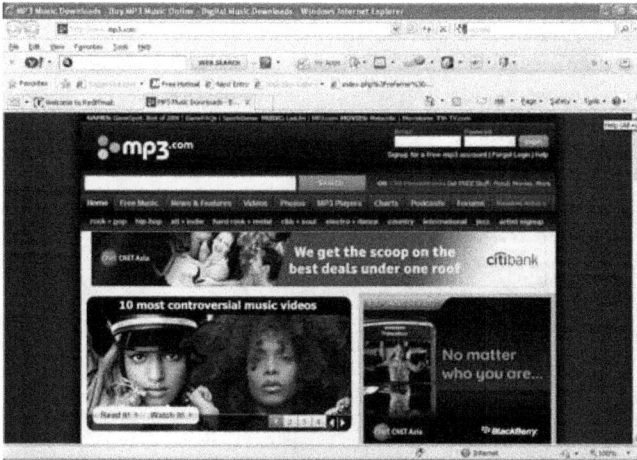

IJigg live.com

This is a great place to find people with similar interests in music. The site allows independent bands to upload their music, so that listeners can download it for free.

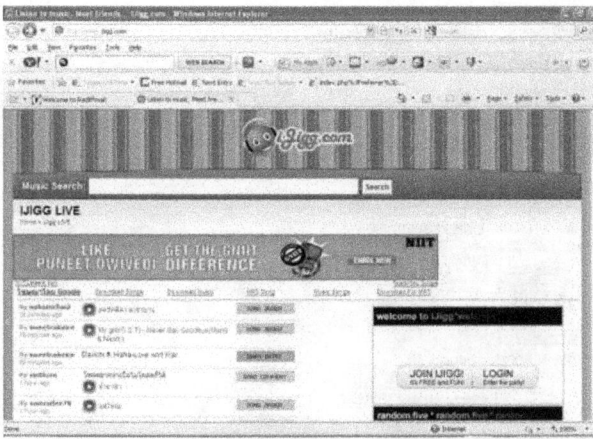

Project Opus**.com**

It is an online community that supports artists, fans and local music. Membership to Project Opus is currently absolutely free.

Muso City.com

The website allows music bands, independent musicians, music venue owners/managers and music retailers to network and connect with each other. Muso city is currently a free to use community.

Midomi.com

The website allows users to actually search for a song by simply humming or singing it. Artists can contribute songs by singing in Midomi's online recording studio. You can join the community for free.

Buzznet.com

This is another popular social networking website dedicated to music fans and artists with lots of features like uploading and sharing photos and videos, etc.

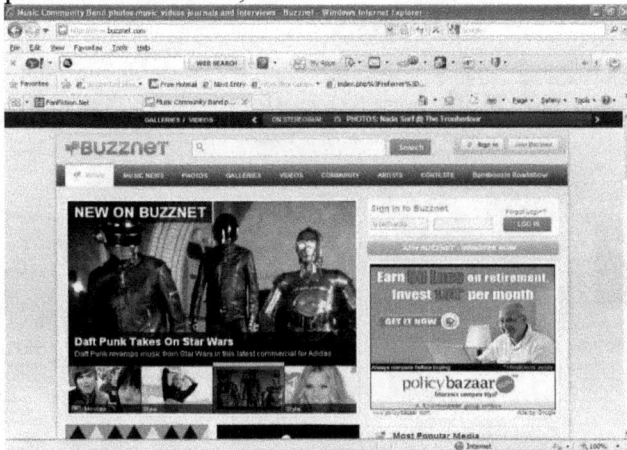

JBA Network.com

This is great way to network and connect with people who are interested in the same type of music or just music in general. You can join JBA for free.

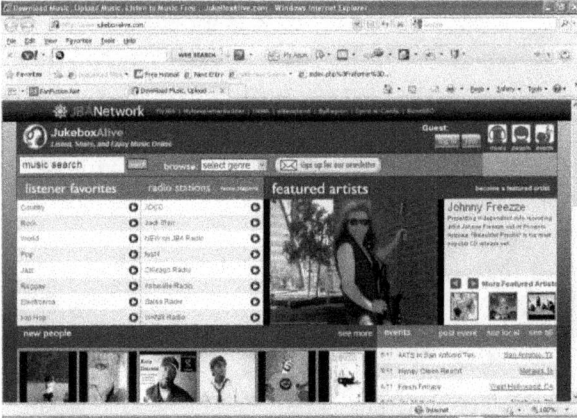

Music Hawk.com

The website is a great place to network with other music lovers. Registration to Music Hawk is currently free.

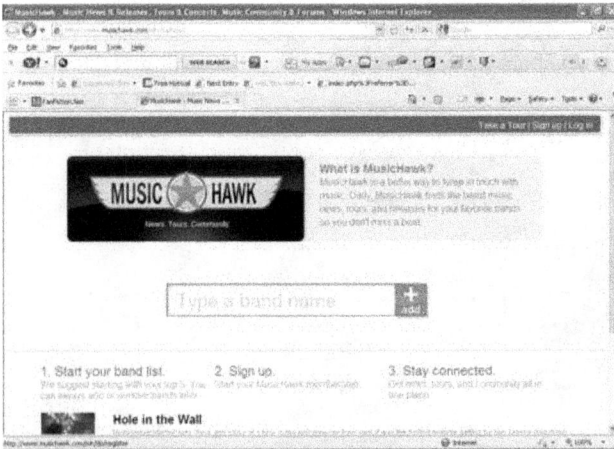

ReverbNation.com

This is a social music network for fans , artists, band managers and music venue owners/managers. Registration to the website is currently free.

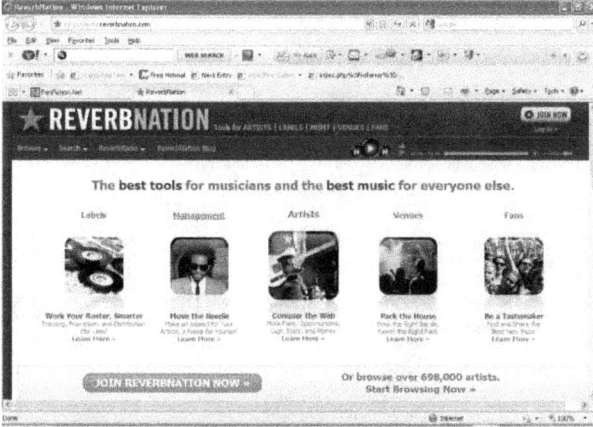

GrooveShark.com

The website allows users to create free internet radio stations and search for their favorite tracks. The site offers both free and VIP (ad free) memberships.

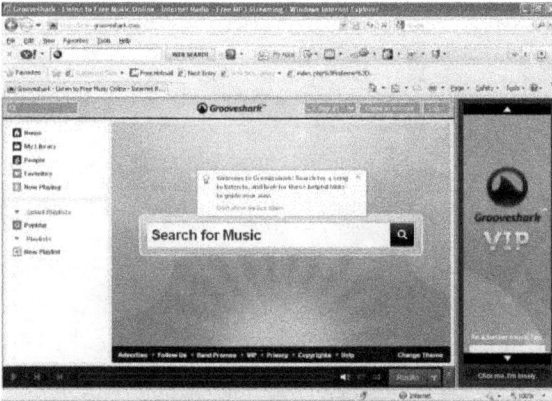

DopeTracks.com

The website is a network of Hip hop artist and producers.
Registration to the website is currently free.

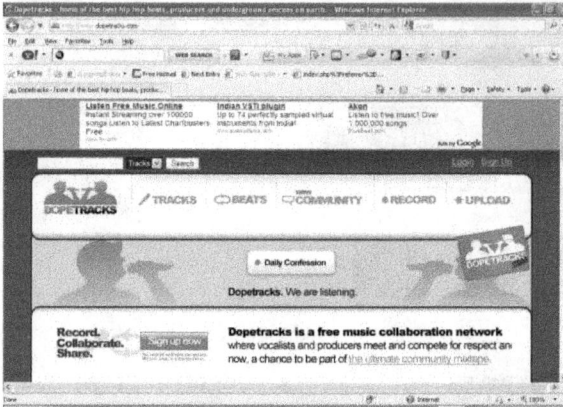

FIQL.com

This is a music network that allows users to upload and share their
original playlists. Registration to the website is currently free.

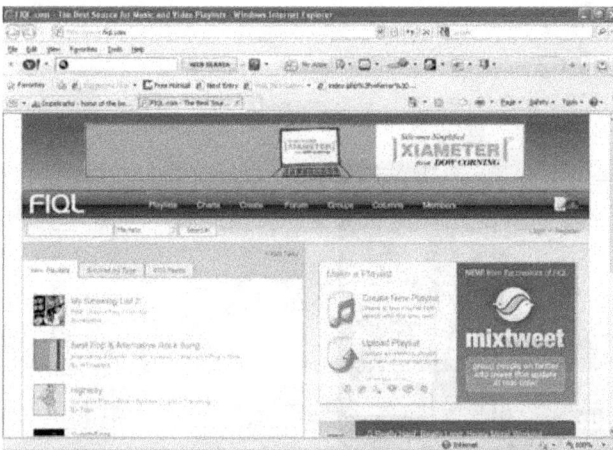

FineTune.com

This is a music based community that allows people to connect with like minded music lovers, browse artists and listen to user created playlists, etc. Registration to FineTune is currently free.

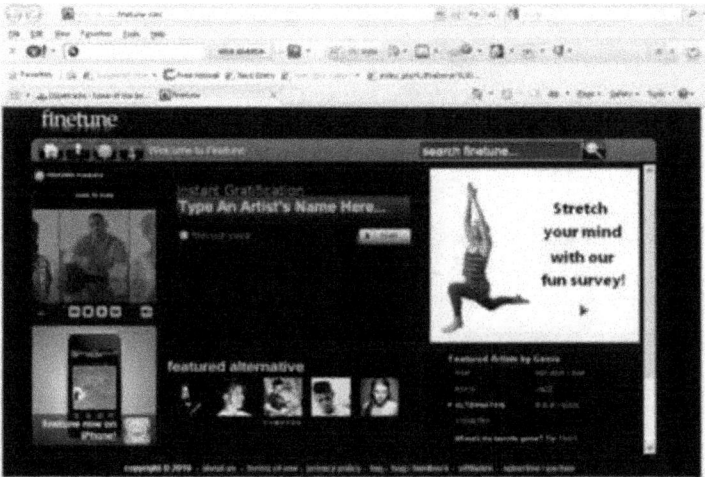

The Sixty One.com

This is a music sharing website that allows artists to upload their music and listeners can search for music by genres, moods, artists, etc. You can sign up to Sixty One for free or log in with your Facebook account.

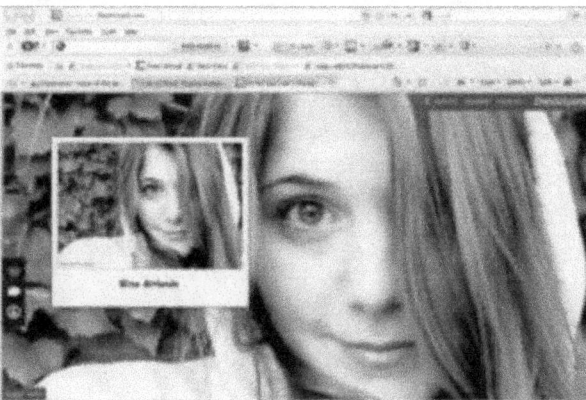

The Hype Machine.com

The website keeps track of what music bloggers write about and presents the best ones to its users. It also allows its users to bookmark songs, artists, music tracks and blogs. Registration to the website is currently free.

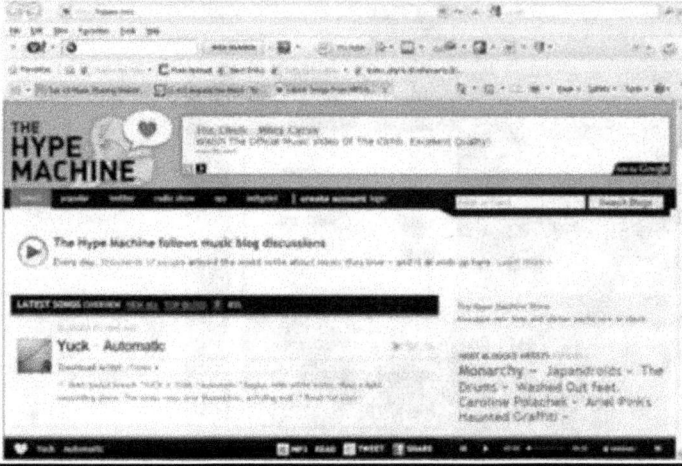

SoundCloud.com

This is another music based networking website that offers a platform to artist to upload their songs. Registration to the website is currently free.

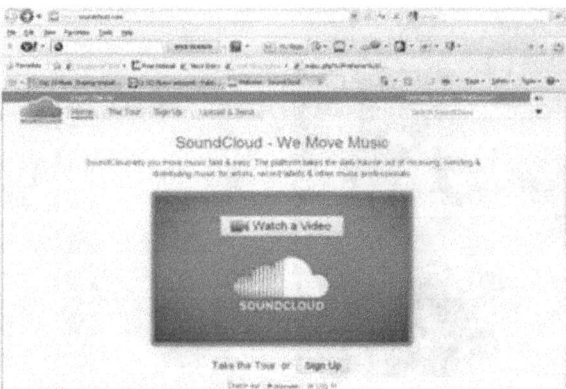

Swift.Fm.com

This is another popular music sharing website that allows users to upload original tracks and music links. You can also search for your favorite music tracks. The network is working towards creating a portal for music labels to discover new artists. You can log in to Swift.Fm with your twitter id.

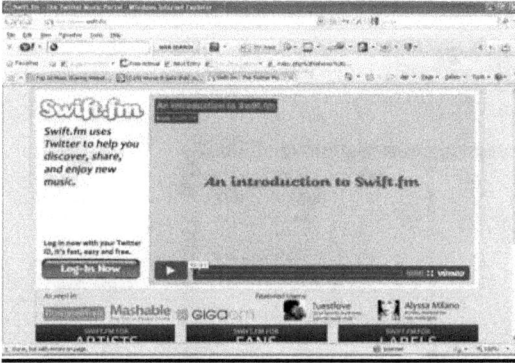

Song.ly

The website allows user to share music on Twitter. You can sign in with you Twitter id.

Twiturm.com

The website allows artists to promote their music through various social networks like Facebook and twitter. You can sign in with you Twitter account.

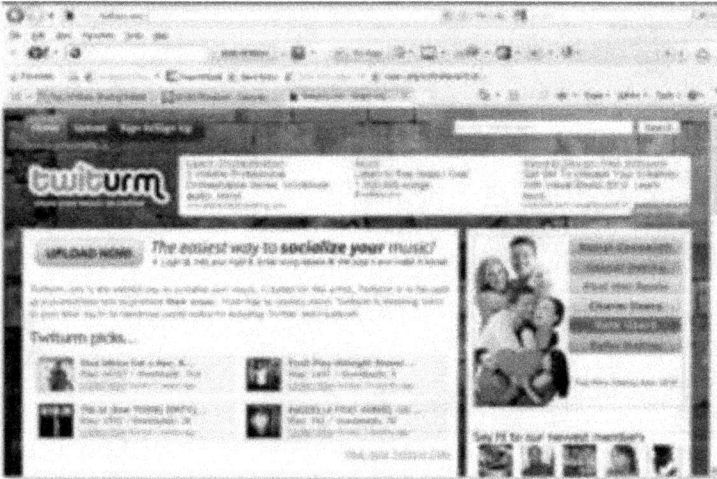

My Space Music.com

This is a social networking website for music lovers. Users can post their original music tracks/videos, interact with each other, discover new artists and comment on each others posts. You can sign up to My Space Music for free.

Chapter 12
On The Go Social Networking Websites

Most social networking websites today provide mobile integration services. However, there are certain websites that focus almost completely on mobile applications or networking through cell phones. From a marketers perspective joining these websites would make a lot of sense if you are in the business of creating mobile applications, have anything to do with cell phones or want to market your product or service to teenagers and young adults.

CrackBerry.com

This is a social networking website for Blackberry users. Registration to Crackberry is currently free.

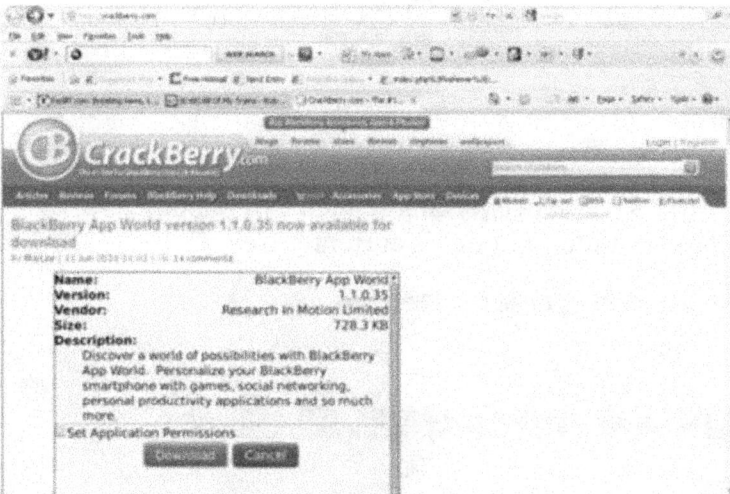

Jaiku.com

The website allows people to stay connected with each other through their cell phones. You can join Jaiku for free.

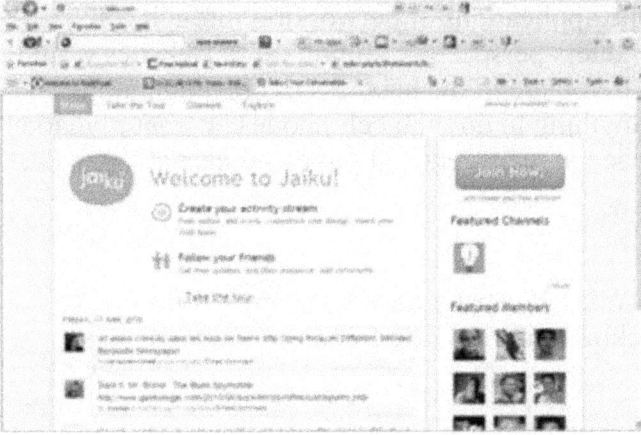

Loopt.com

The website offers several networking related cell phone applications. Registration to Loopt is currently free.

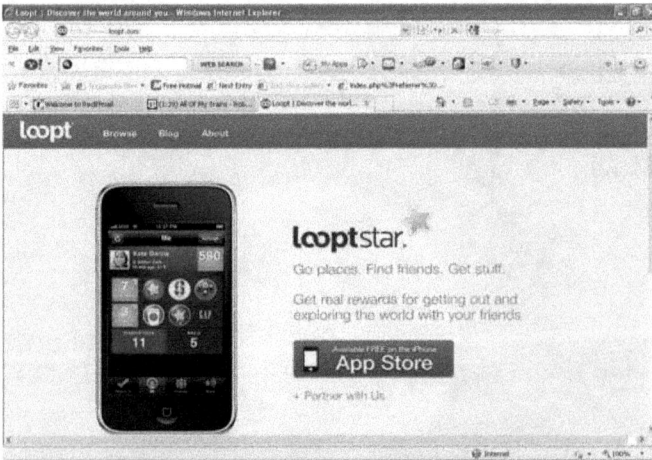

Mobango.com

This is a great place for mobile applications developers to build their brand and for users to get mobile applications, games and ringtones, etc.

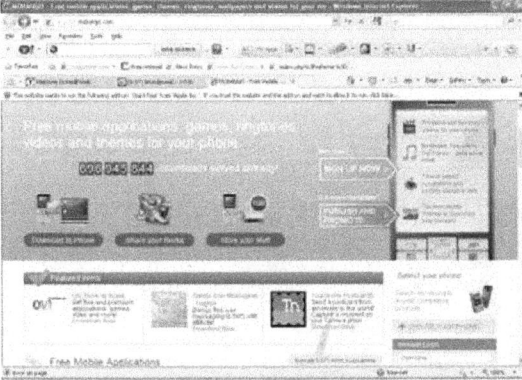

Mozes.com

The website provides a pay to use web based platform to businesses through which they can engage their customers on their mobile phones through activities related to music, sports, entertainment and social/environmental causes.

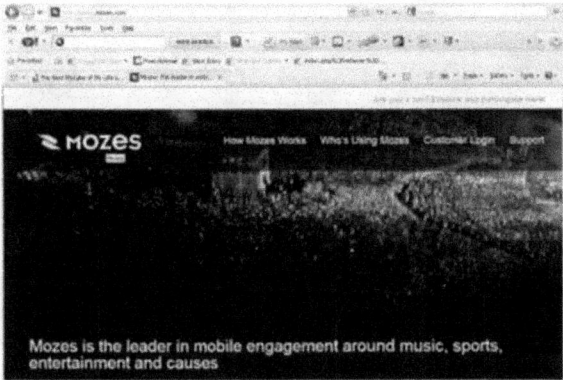

Mozes is the leader in mobile engagement around music, sports, entertainment and causes

Peepsnation.com

This is a mobile social networking application designed especially for teenagers and young adults with similar interests. Registration to Peepsnation is free.

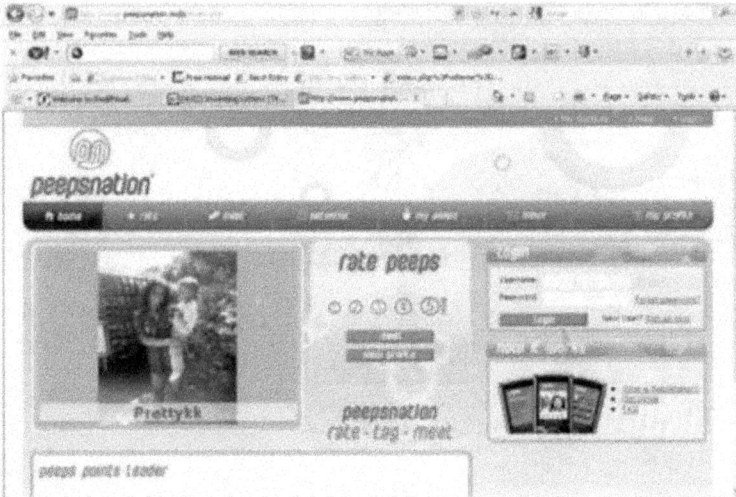

SociaLight.com

Socialight is a pay to use service that lets users create their own mobile applications and communities around location-based content.

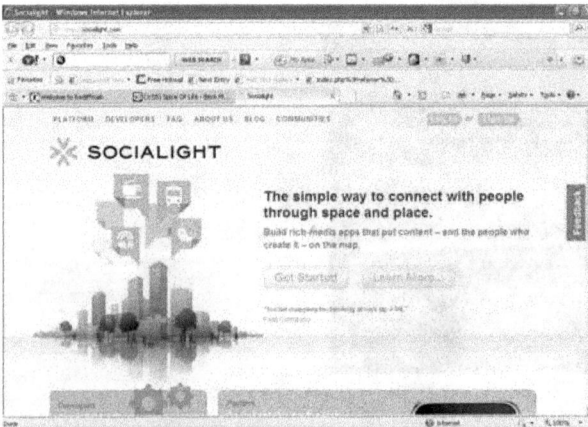

Wattpad.com

This is a mobile based social network that allows users to share original stories, e-books, fan fictions, etc, with each other.

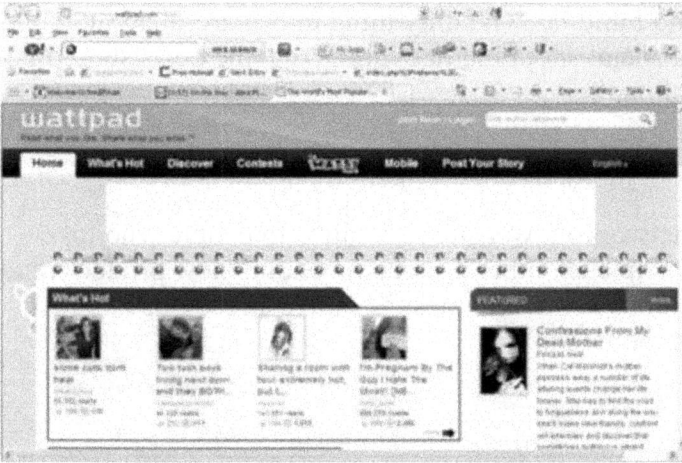

Chapter 13
Social Shopping Networking Sites

We are all here to sell something, right? So what's better than joining social shopping networks! These networks offer marketers an insight into their customer's psyche and provide an excellent platform for brand building. The only thing to be careful about while participating in a social shopping network is that the posts should not sound too promotional.

Kaboodle.com

This is a social networking website that caters to people who love shopping. Users help each other by recommending new products and sharing their opinions about the ones they have already used. Registration to Kaboodle is free.

The website allows users to get great bargains on several cool items. Woot puts one product on sale daily until it's sold out or until 11:59pm central time and then replaces it by the next day's item.

This Next.com

The website provides users a platform to discuss the products they like.

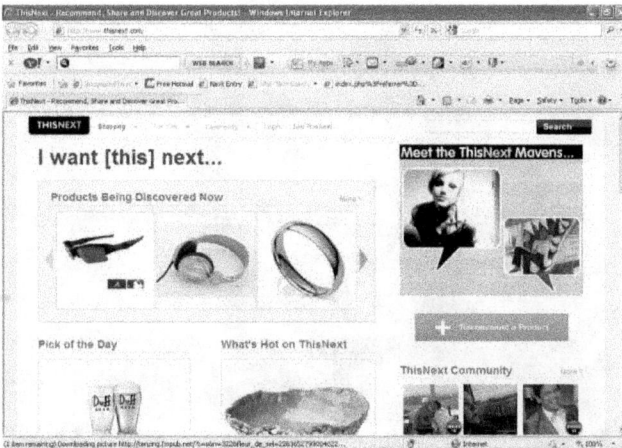

Buzillions.com

The website allows like minded shoppers connect with each other and post product reviews.

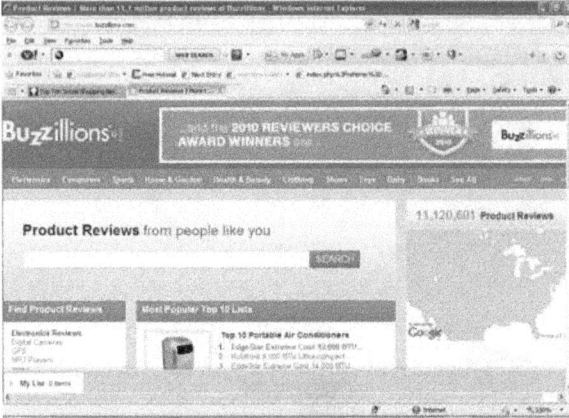

3Luxe

The website makes shopping easier for users by recommending the three best products in all kinds of categories. Registration to 3Luxe is free.

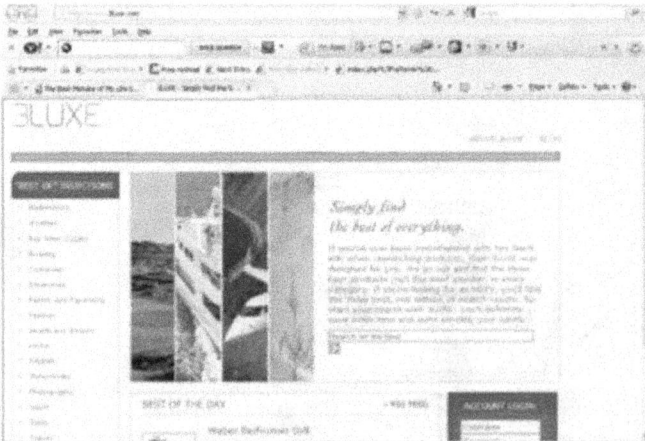

AgentB.com

This is a social network where people share information about the best deals on the web with each other. You can join Agent B for free.

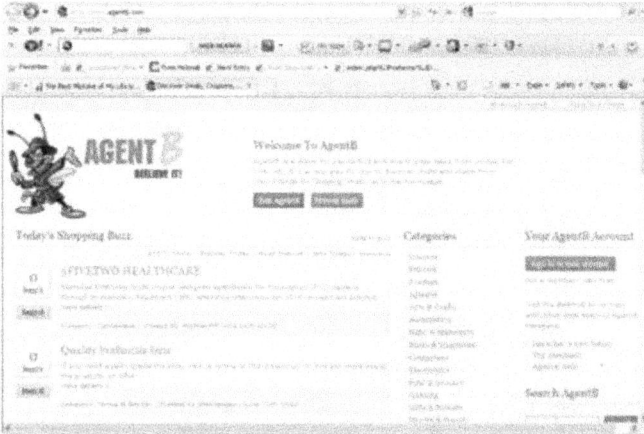

Bringsome.com

This is a p2p delivery platform that allows users get access the best goodies across the globe. Registration to Bring some is currently free.

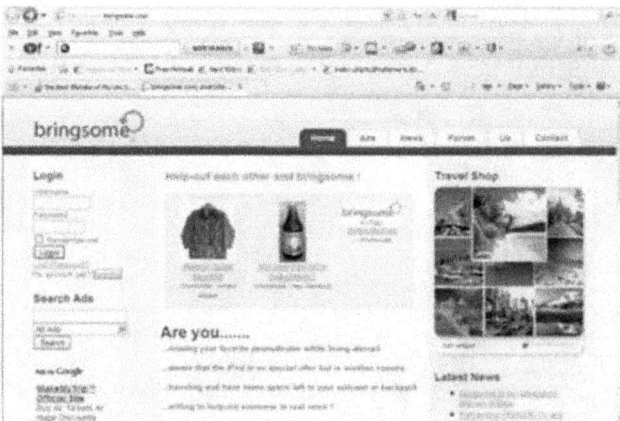

Boxed Up.com

The network allows users to bookmark, rate and share information about products that they like. You can sign up to the website for free.

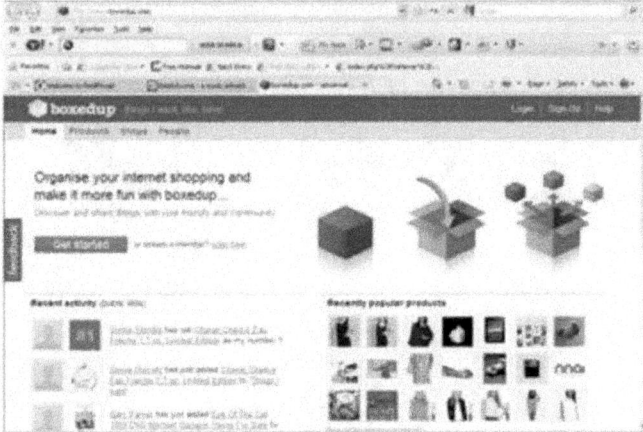

Iliketotallyloveit.com

This is another website where users share information about the products they like, love or would love to buy. Registration to Iliketotallyloveit is free.

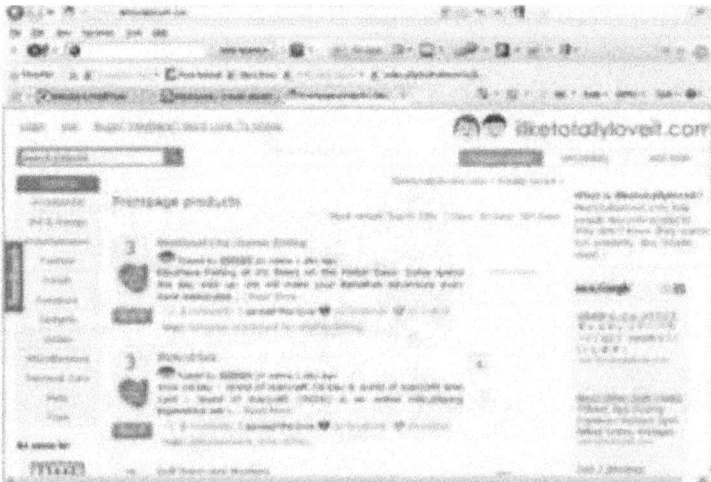

MyItThings.com

This is a community where people share their shopping finds, wish lists as well as opinions and views about fashion brands as well as the latest beauty and fashion trends. You can sign up to the website for free.

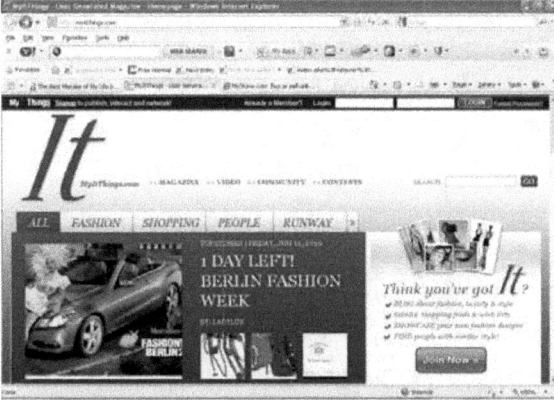

Mystore.com

This is a social network that allows people to buy and sell their products. Registration to the website is currently free; however, you'll have to pay for using premium services.

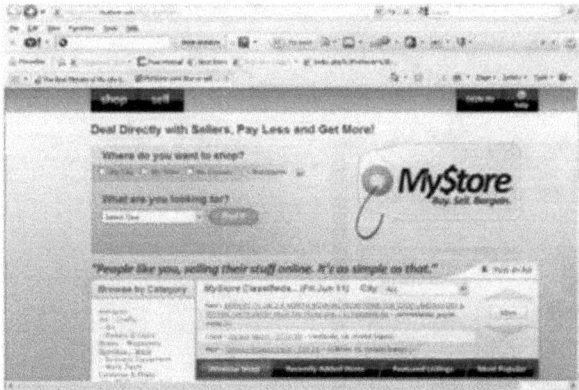

RedFlag.com

This is one of Canada's most popular bargain hunting communities. Registration to the website is currently free.

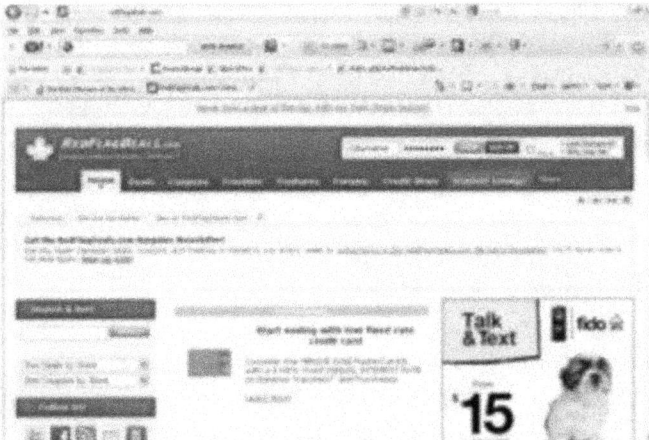

ChickAdvisor.com

This networking website is a social platform for women in North America to share their opinions about women's products and services available in the market. You can sign up to the website for free.

Fiverr.com

This is the online version of the dollar store, only it's a five dollar store. Fiverr is a website where you can buy products and services for $5.

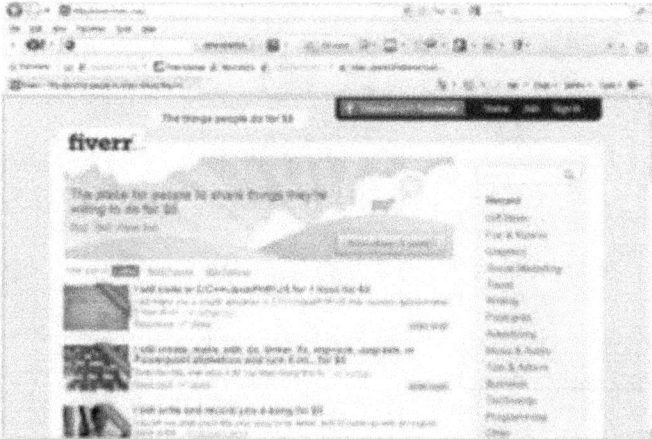

Ideeli.com

This is a members-only shopping community that offers current fashion products at great prices. Membership to the site is currently free.

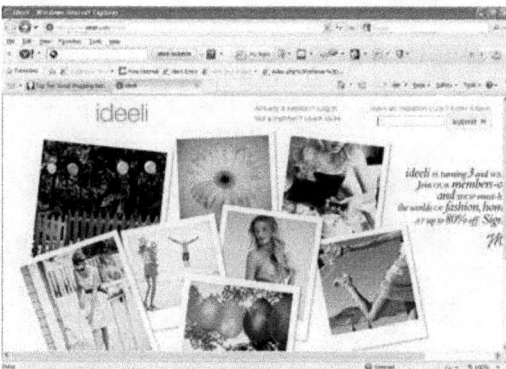

Stylefeeder.com

This is a social shopping site where you can virtually rub shoulders with celebs. The site provides users a unique style search engine that can actually 'learn' their personal style.

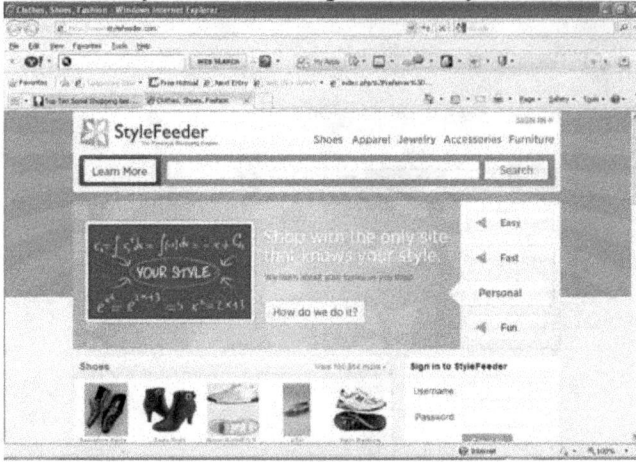

Chapter 14
Social Bookmarking and Networking Sites

These are the sites you would want to submit your content to. We have already discussed social bookmarking sites in detail, so all I am going to say is, go through these sites carefully and choose the ones you like best.

I have also listed some bookmark management tools that should make your job of spreading links across these websites easier. Good luck.

Stumble upon.com

This is an intelligent social bookmarking platform that recommends additional sites to users based on their likes.

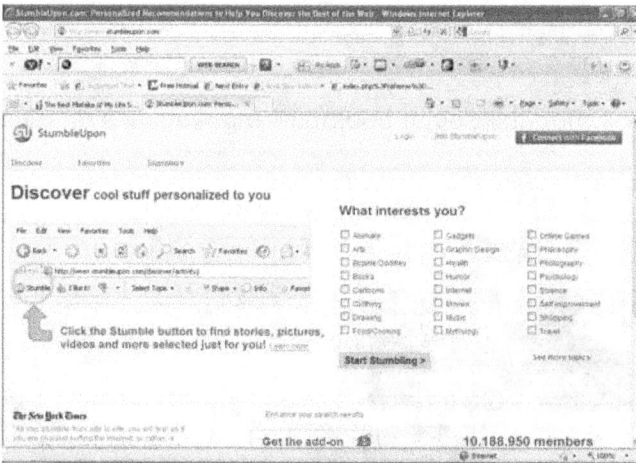

Delicious.com

The website hardly needs any introduction after all it is one of the
Big Boys in the social bookmarking world.

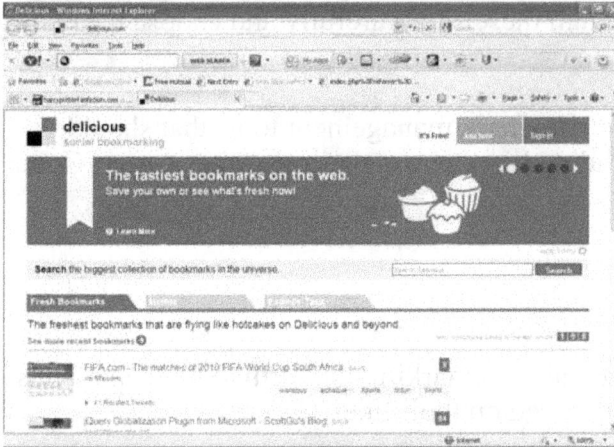

Digg.com

Digg is one of the most popular social bookmarking websites on the
net.

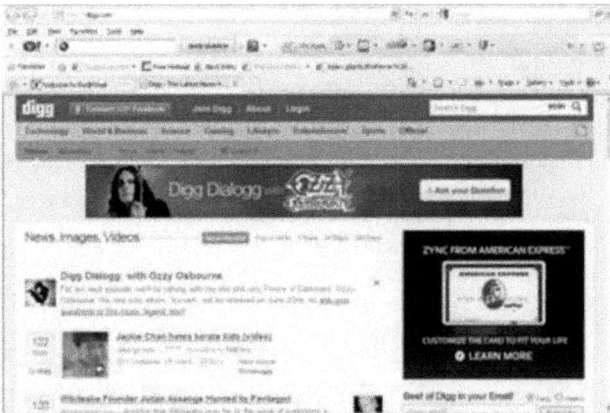

Technorati.com

This website allows real-time search for user-generated content by tags or keywords. If you have a blog registration on this site is a must.

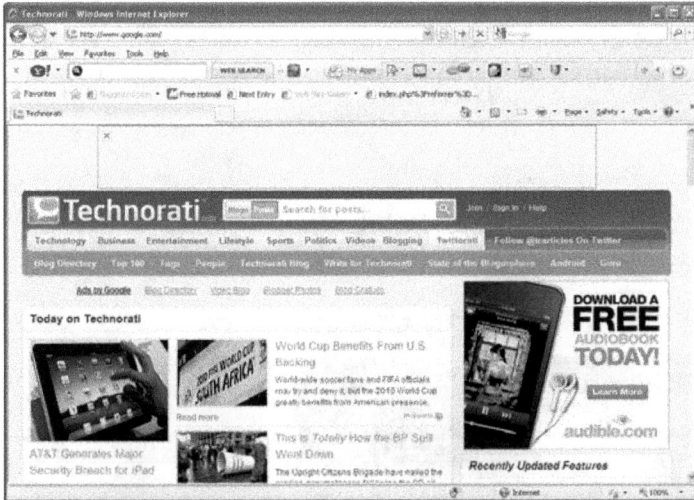

Diigo.com

This is a virtual sticky note bookmarking service that allows users to make notes on their archived web pages.

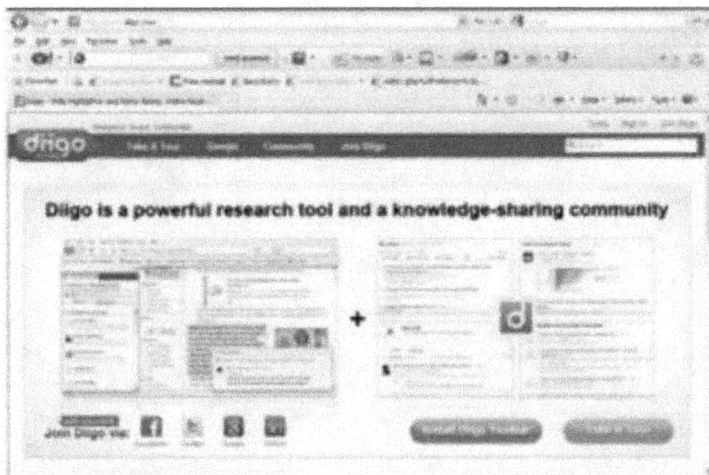

Shoutwire

This is a community based online news website, i.e.the conetnt on the site is regulated by community members instead of an editor. You can sign up for free and submit your aticles, pictures, videos and blogs.

i89.US

This is an easy to use bookmark management and exporting website.

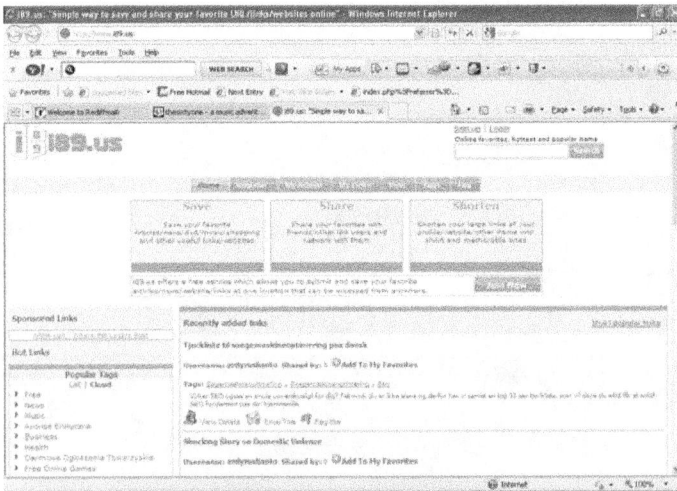

AllMyFavorites.com

This is a social bookmarking website that allows users to create a webpage of all their favorite links.

Blink Pro

BlinkPro is a pay to use service that allows users to manage their bookmarks, protect them from system crashes and access their links from any computer anywhere. The site offers a free 30 days trial.

Blogmarks.com

This is a by invitation only social bookmarking service.

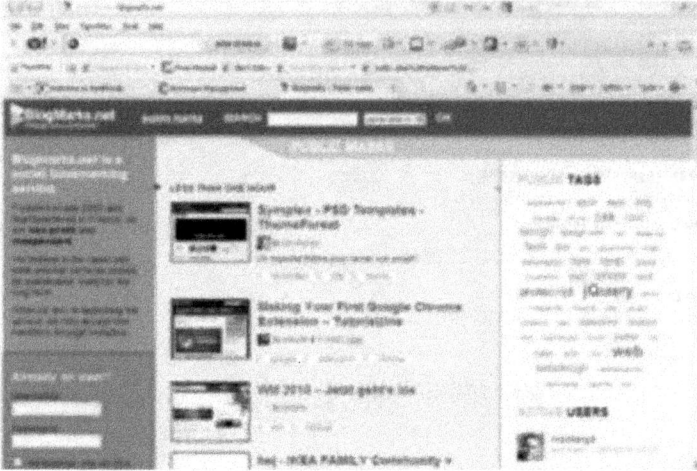

BuddyMarks.com

This is an easy to use social bookmarking service.

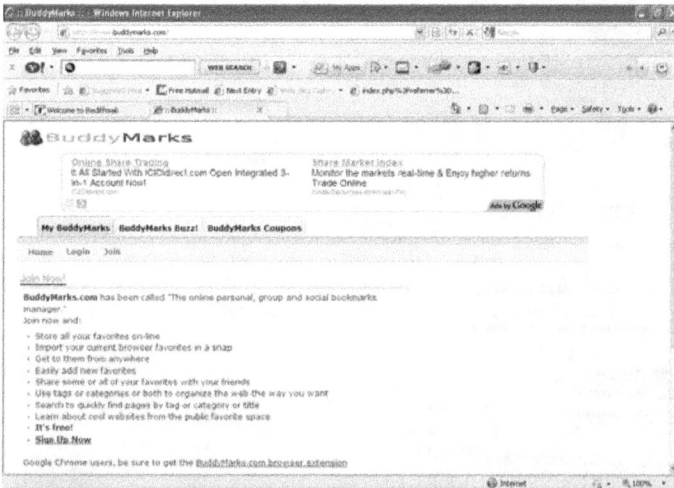

Chipmark.com

The site offers useful tools to manage your bookmarks and explore those saved by others.

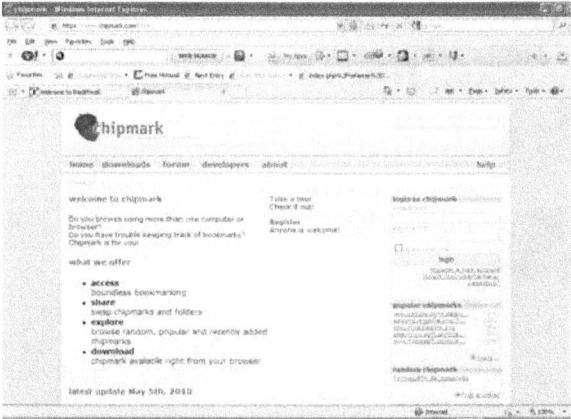

Connotea.com

This is a bookmarking service specially designed for scientists and researchers.

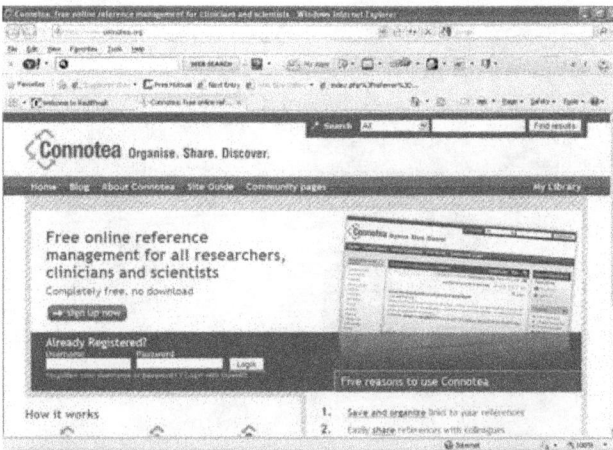

Givealink.org

The website allows users to share their bookmarks and download the Firefox extension to organize and share links using social maps. Givealink is also planning to introduce a new feature that will make it easier for users to create social links across the web.

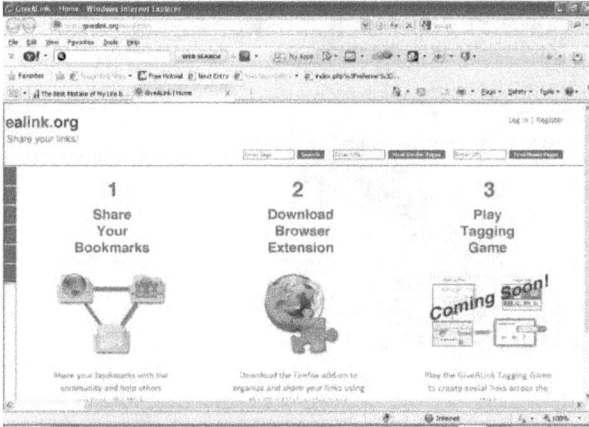

Ikeepbookmarks.com

This is an easy to use social bookmarking service.

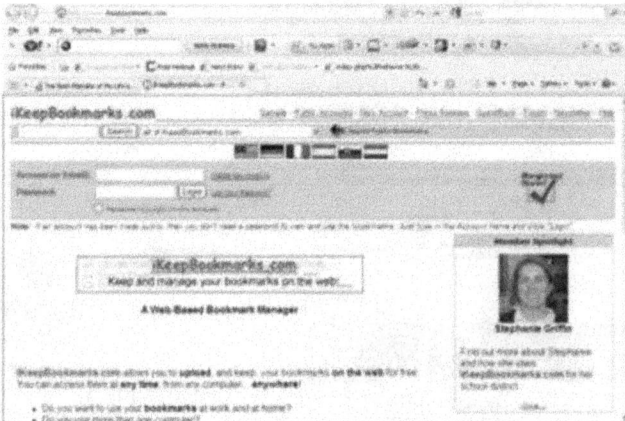

Linkroll.com

This is a social bookmarking service that allows users to save links to their favorite pages and comment on other people's bookmarks.

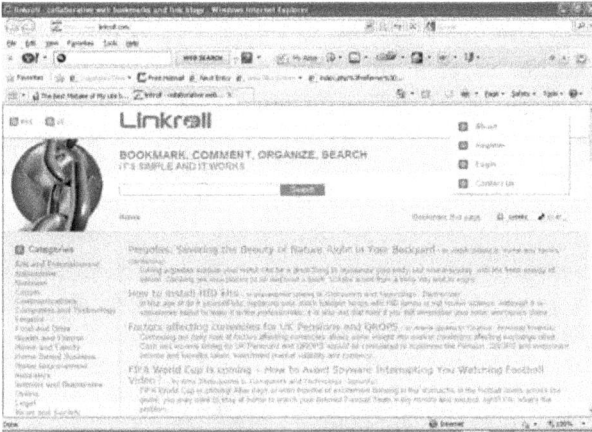

Mister Wong.com

This easy to use bookmarking site is integrated with Twitter so that users can automatically import interesting links.

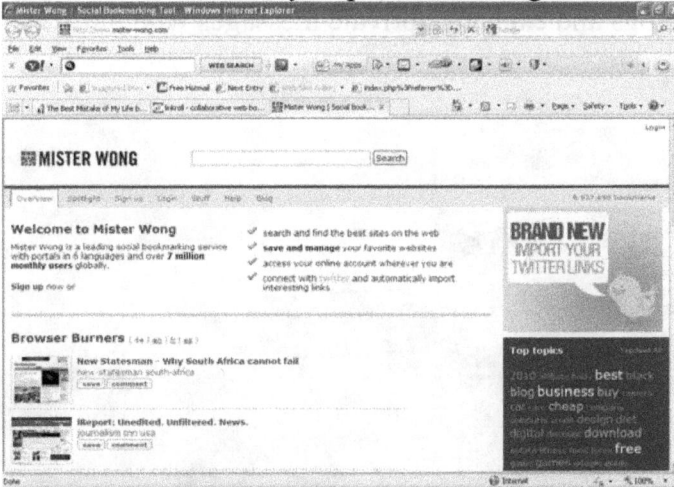

Netvouz.com

This bookmarking service is easy to use and also offers password protection features for added privacy.

Nextaris.com

This is a powerful social bookmarking service that allows users to keep track of their favorite websites, capture web content, share files, publish weblogs and exchange private messages with other users.

WireFan.com

This is a simple and easy to use social bookmarking site.

BlinkList.com

Blink list is a popular social bookmarking site that literally allows users to save their bookmarks in the blink of an eye.

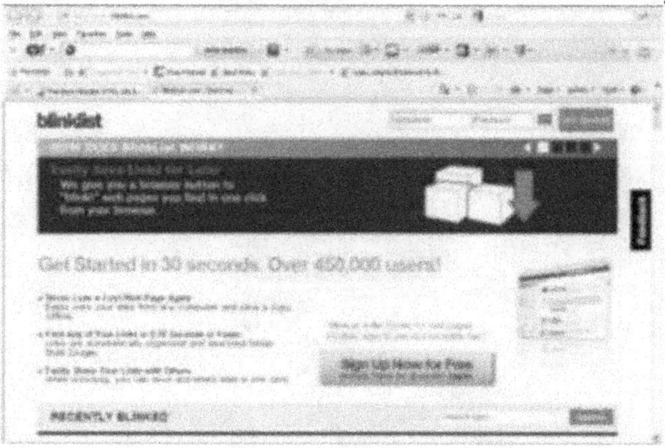

Clip Clip.com

This social bookmarking is like an online scarp book as it actually allows users to share specific parts of websites with people.

Clip Marks.com

The social bookmarking website allows users to clip parts of websites that they like and insert them to their blogs.

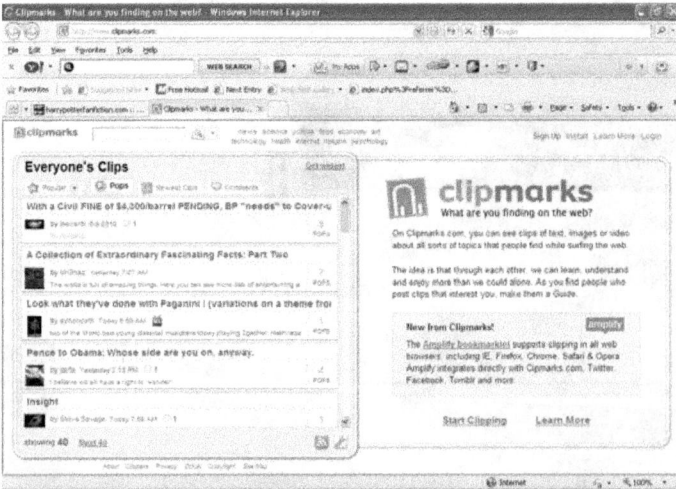

Linkatopia.com

This is a simple and easy to use social bookmarking service.

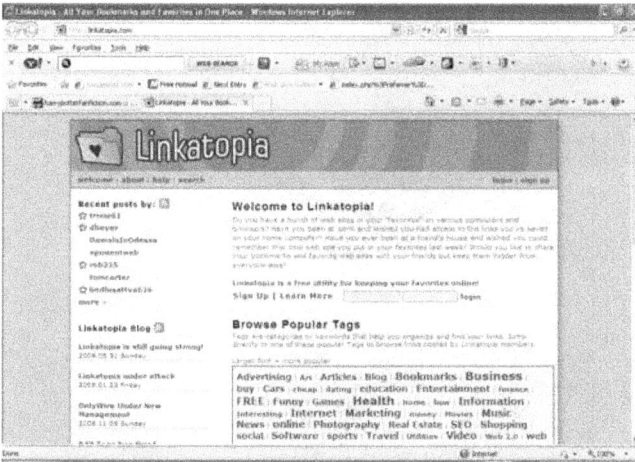

Simpy.com

This is a social bookmarking service that lets users save, tag, search and share their bookmarks, groups and notes.

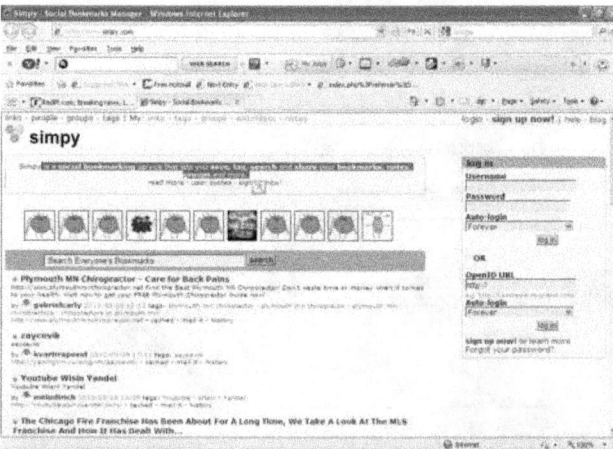

Spurl.net

This is an easy to use social bookmarking service and search engine.

Newsvine.com

This is a user controlled news and information website.

Reddit.com

This is another user controlled website where content is regulated by votes from members.

Bit.ly

This website provides an easy to use tool that allows users to shorten and share their links.

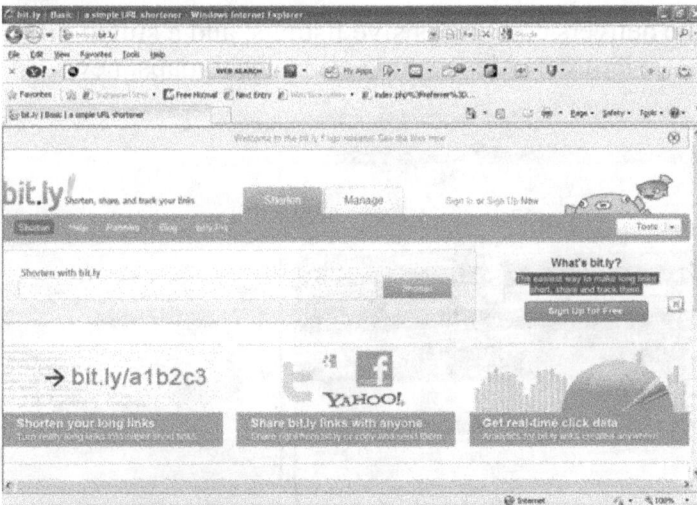

Social Marker.com

This is a powerful free social bookmarking tool that spreads a link to 50 top social bookmarking websites in under 15 minutes!

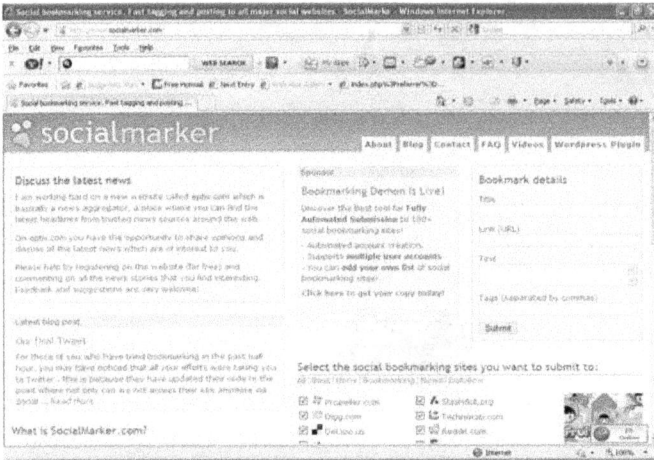

Netscape

www.netscape.aol.com

The search engine delivers comprehensive listings, and a single-click access to relevant, pictures, videos sound clips, local maps, news, etc.

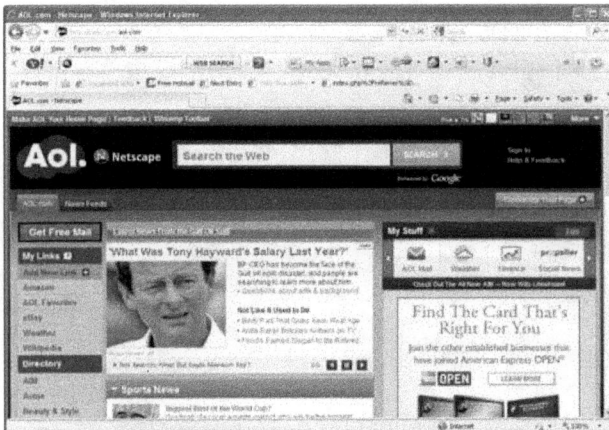

Raw Sugar.com

This search engine makes navigation easier and helps users find the exact information that they are looking for.

Squidoo.com

This is a popular publishing platform and community that makes it easy for you to create "lenses" online. Lenses are like brief summaries that catch the gist of an article.

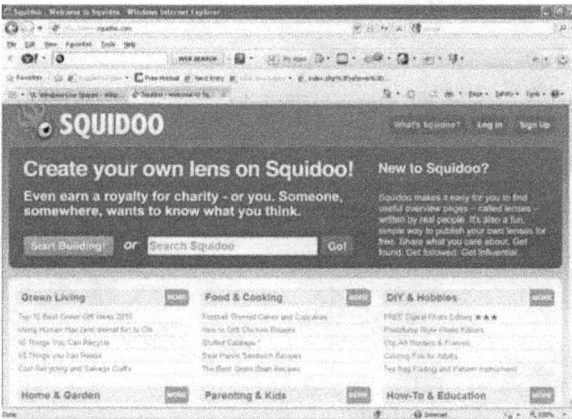

Gnolia.com

This is an online community that focuses on link saving and sharing. Currently membership is by invitation only.

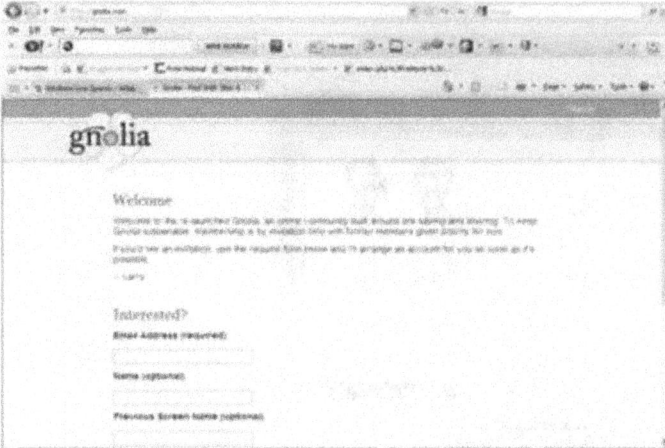

TagTooga.com

This is another easy to use social bookmarking website.

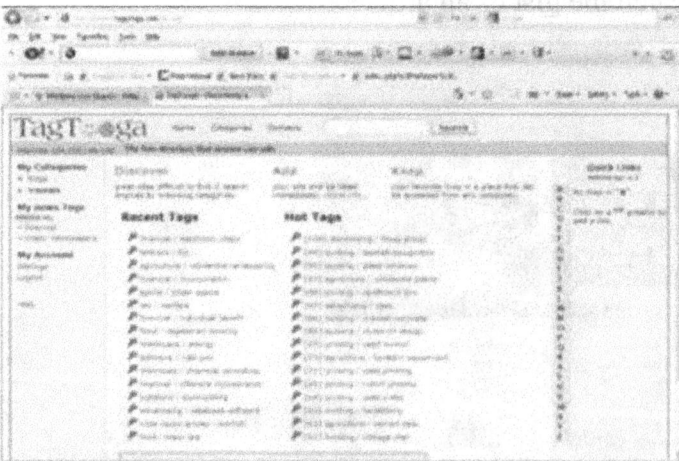

Ask.com

This is a popular search engine that hardly needs any introduction. You can find relevant information with a simple click.

Chapter 15

College and High School Social Networking Websites

If you have a product or service that young people may be interested in, these sites will lead you straight to your target market! Remember not to sound too promotional or businesslike after your join these networks, as that may put some users off.

Classmates.com

This social networking website can help users who studied in Canada, USA, Australia, France, Germany, Sweden and Overseas American and Canadian Schools, stay in touch with their classmates. You can sign up to the website for free but will have to pay for using premium services.

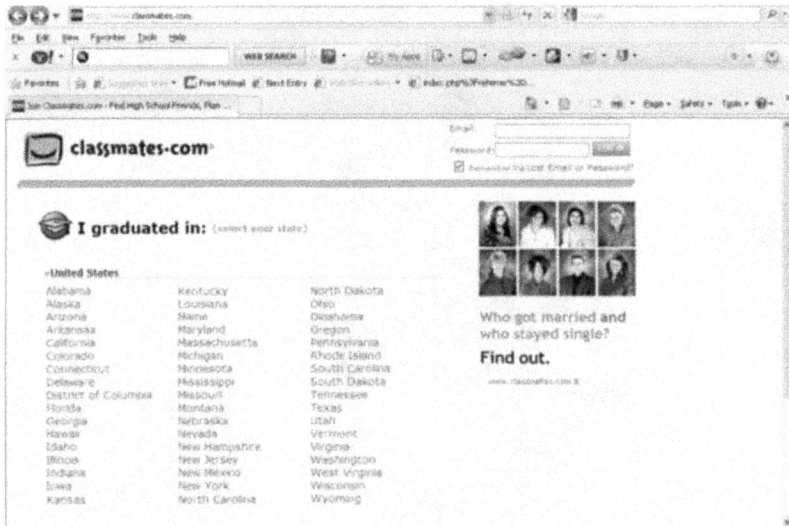

Fledge Wing.com

This is an online community for entrepreneurial students looking for success in their careers.

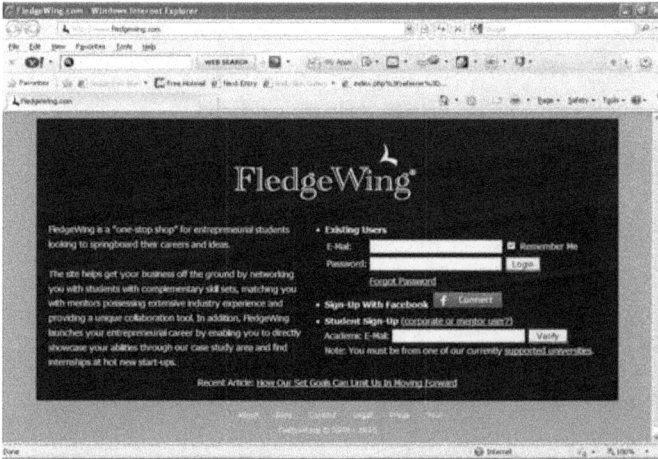

Alumwire.com

This social network makes it easier for college students to find jobs by networking and connecting with their alumni and recruiters.

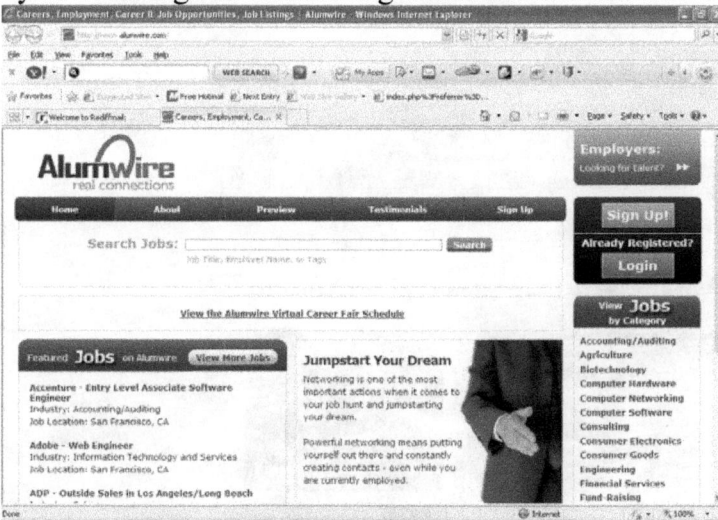

Campusburg.com

The website provides educational and social networking tools to students all over the world.

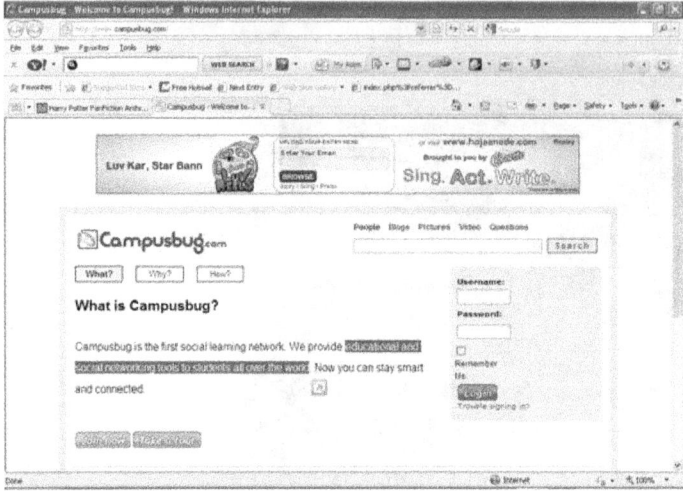

CollegeMedium.com

College students can post ads and look for jobs, flat mates, used books, etc, through this networking website.

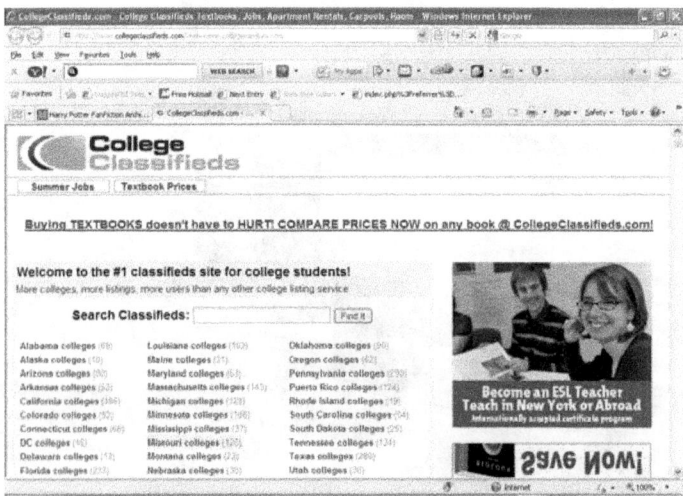

Graduates.com

This is a social networking website that allows college students to stay in touch with their classmates after graduation.

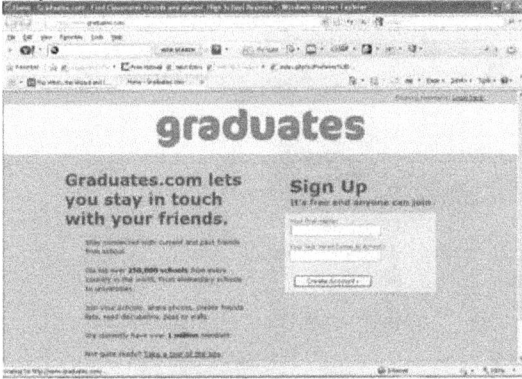

Half.com

The website allows college students to buy and sell used college text books online.

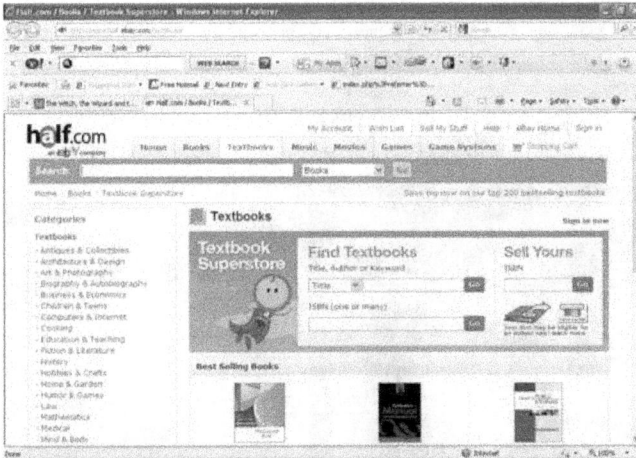

Ihipo.com

The networking website is designed to help college students find
International jobs and internships.

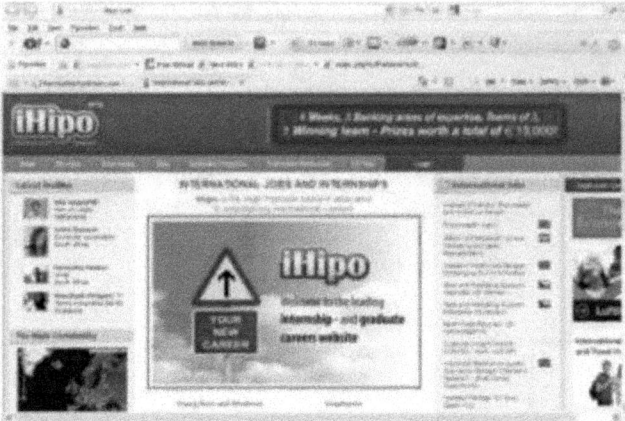

Localschools.com

This networking website helps students locate local schools and get
information on them.

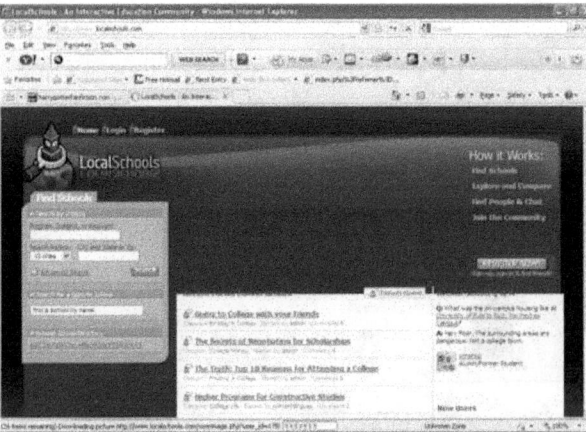

College Banana**.com**

This website helps students prepare for their campus life by helping them network with college seniors.

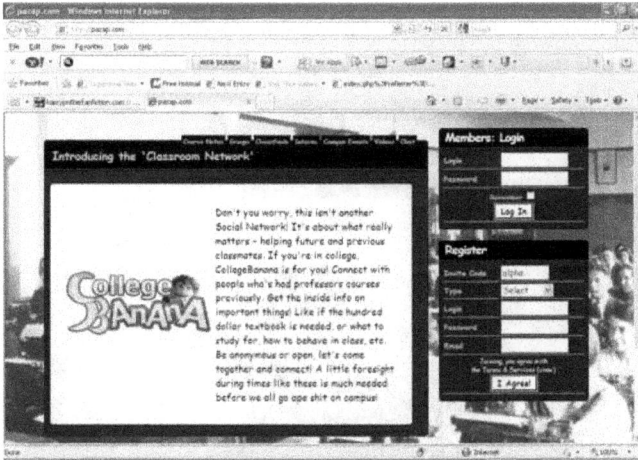

Quizzila
www.quizilla.teennick.com

This networking website allows users to create and share great content like stories, quizzes, poetry, blogs, etc. Most of the site's members are teenagers and young adults.

Rate My Professors.com

The website offers college students a platform to discuss college related subjects and rate their teachers/professors.

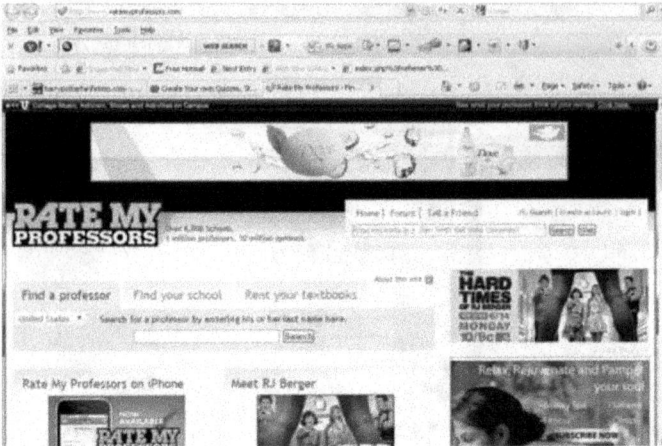

Student.com

This is a popular resource and networking site for college and high school students.

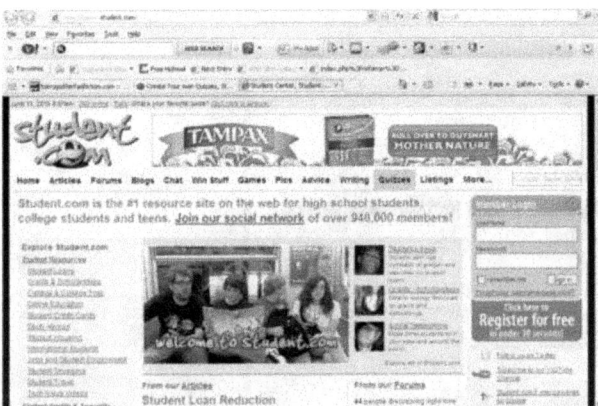

Uloop.com

This website allows students to post information about events, gigs, jobs, housing, etc and also trade used books.

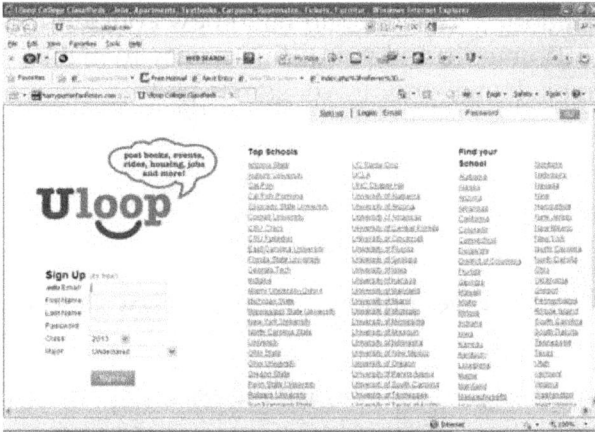

Chapter 16
Vacation and Travel Social Networking Sites

Joining travel based social networking websites does not only make sense for those who work in the travel and tourism industry, but also for those seeking to expand their network and build new contacts. Travel is a great conversation topic and you'll find it easy to make new relationships as you exchange your travel stories and experiences.

Wikitravel
www.wikitravel.org

This is on of the most popular travel information and review sharing networks on the net.

City and Out.com

The website allows users to share travel related information about European cities.

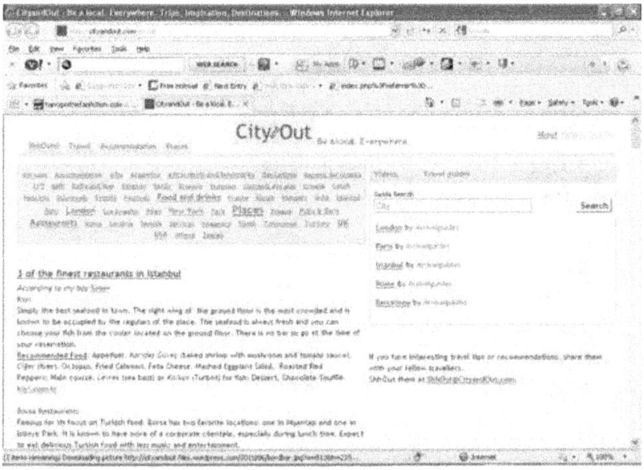

Going.com

The website offers users a platform to share information about New York's night life, events and gigs, etc.

Ioho.com

The websites offers a platform for like minded travelers to network with each other, so that they can plan a great vacation to any destination in the world.

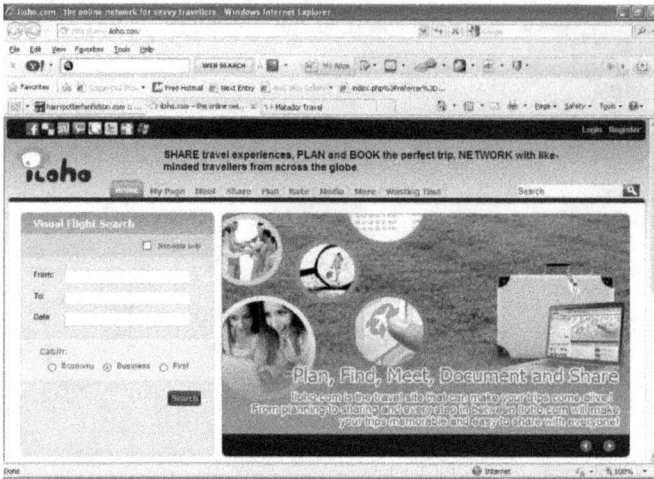

Matador.com

This is an International community for travelers, photographers, writers, adventurers, and grass-roots organizations

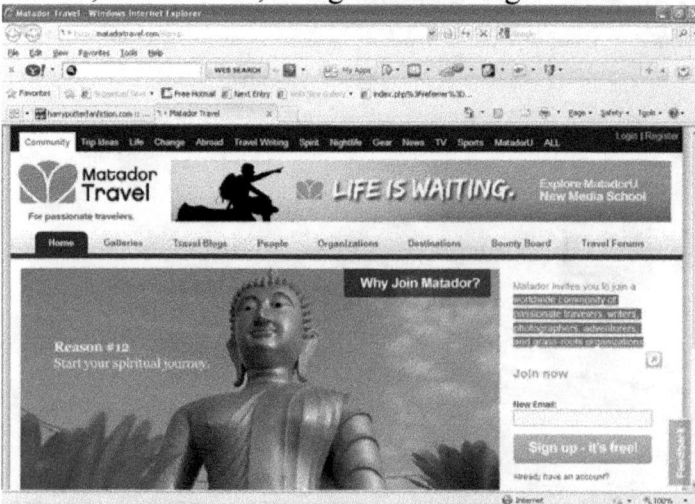

MytripBook.com

The website offers a platform for users to share their travel stories
and photos.

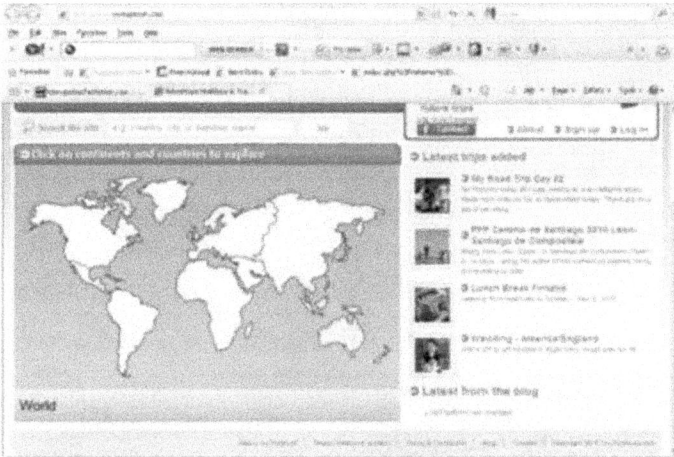

OurFaves.com

This is a travel based social network that offers users a platform to
share information about the best places in Toronto.

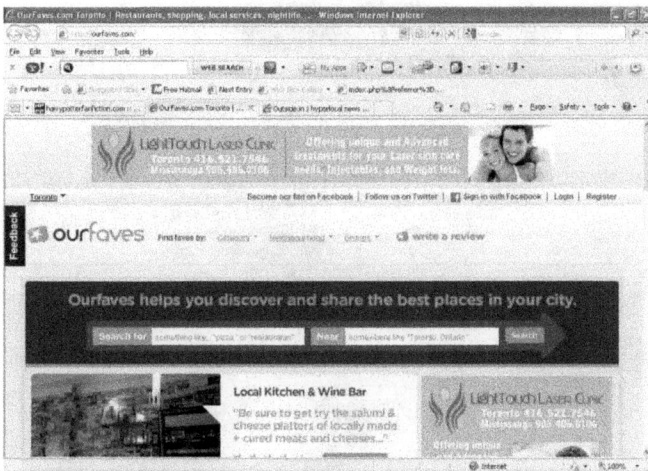

Outside.in

This website helps users keep up to date with current and local happenings in their neighborhoods.

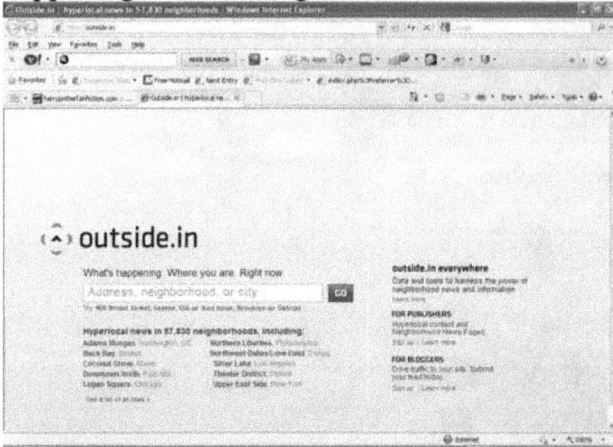

Rumble.com

The social network offers users a platform to rate and review different locations in the world.

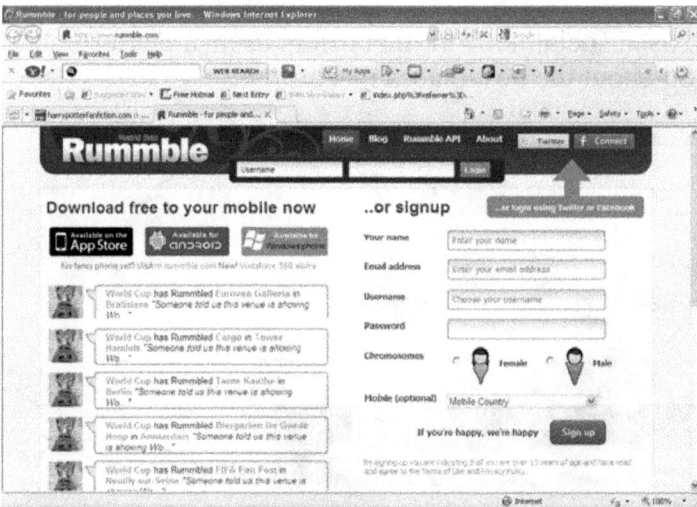

TravBuddy.com

This is an online community for meeting travelers and sharing travel reviews, photos and blogs.

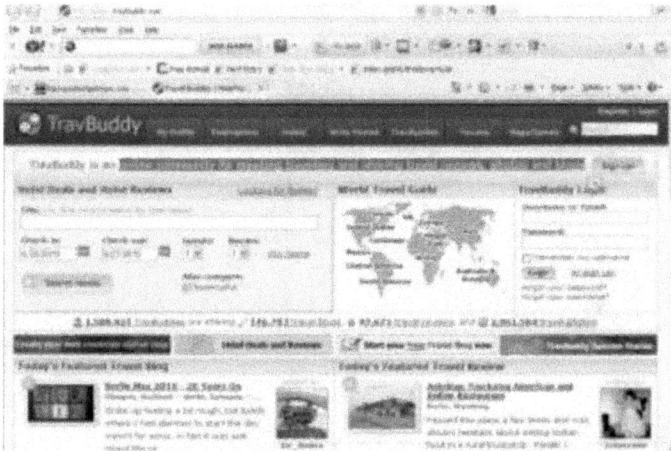

TravellersPoint.com

This is an online community where people can share their travel experiences.

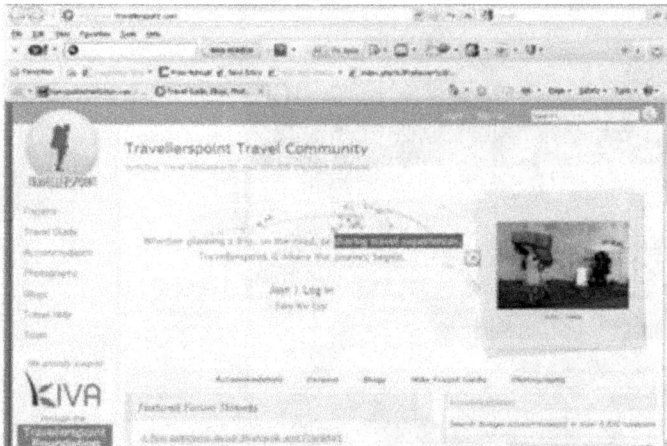

TravelTogether.com

This is another travel based social network where users can swap their travel stories and experiences.

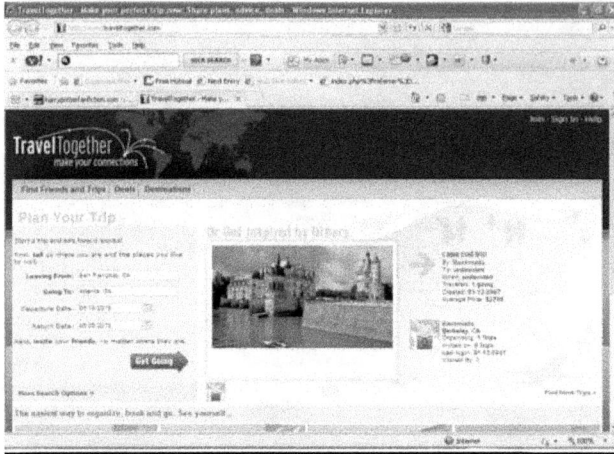

Triporama.com

This is a social network that offers people a platform to find like minded travel partners/buddies.

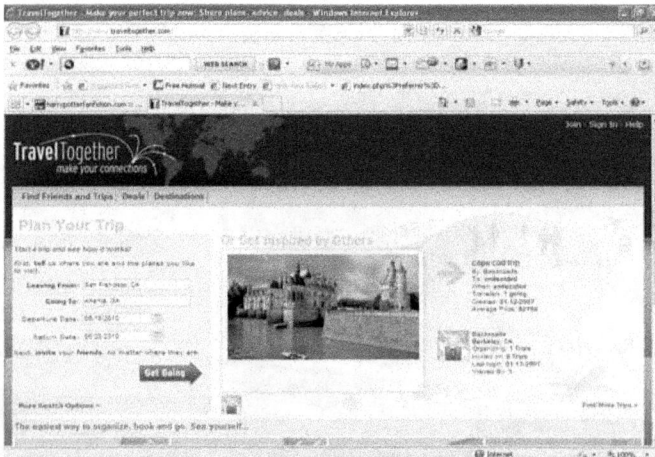

Hotelicopter.com

This online community offers users a platform to share hotel reviews.

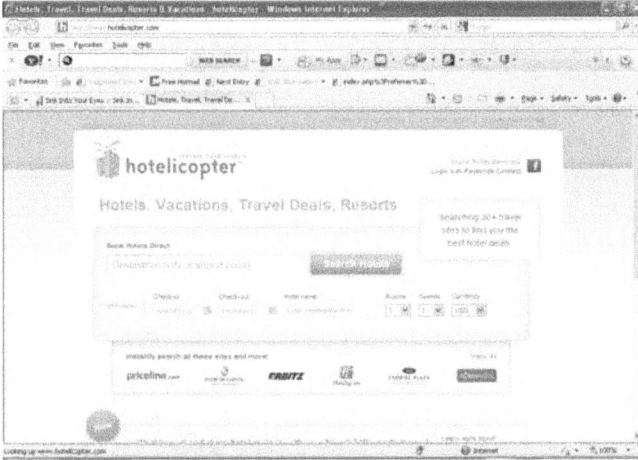

Wayn
www.wayn.com/waynsplash.html

This is another travel based networking site that offers users a platform to share travel stories and connect with like minded people.

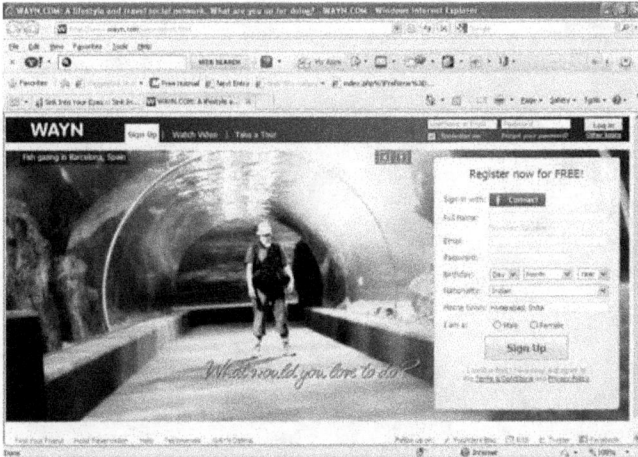

Geopage.com

The website offers interactive map and location-based search features and several other social media tools.

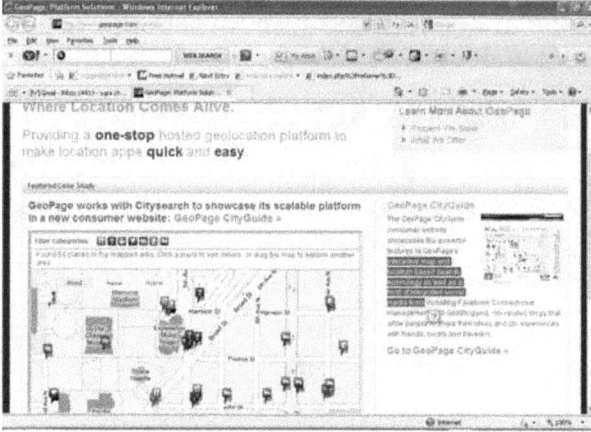

Chapter 17
Social Networking Book Sites

These websites offer an excellent platform to expand your network if you enjoy reading. You can form new relationships as you swap and discuss books with like minded people. These sites can also be useful for aspiring authors.

Shelfari.com

This is one of the most popular social networks for book lovers on the web.

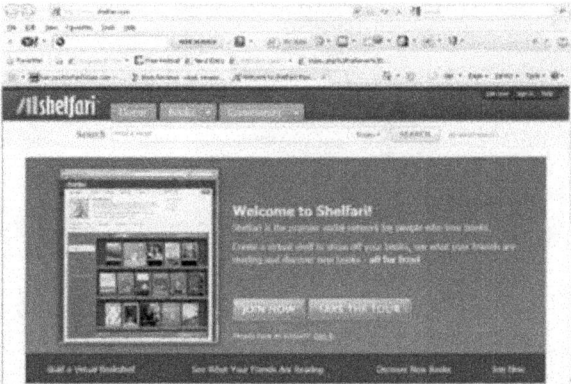

BookConnect
www.countrybookshop.co.uk

This is a community of publishers, readers and librarians, etc, who enjoy reading and reviewing books.

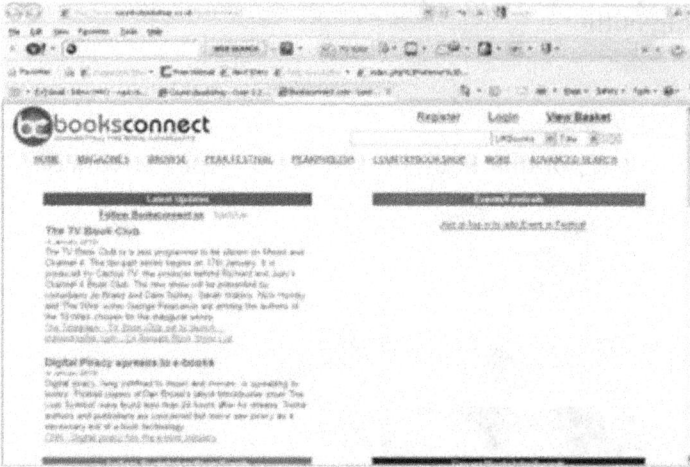

BookCrossing.com

This is a platform where booklovers can share their books and connect with like minded book lovers.

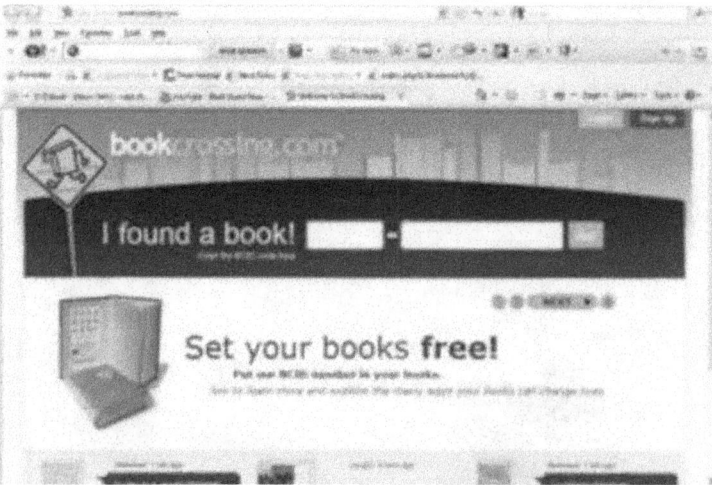

BookHopper.com

The site allows UK based users to share and swap their books.

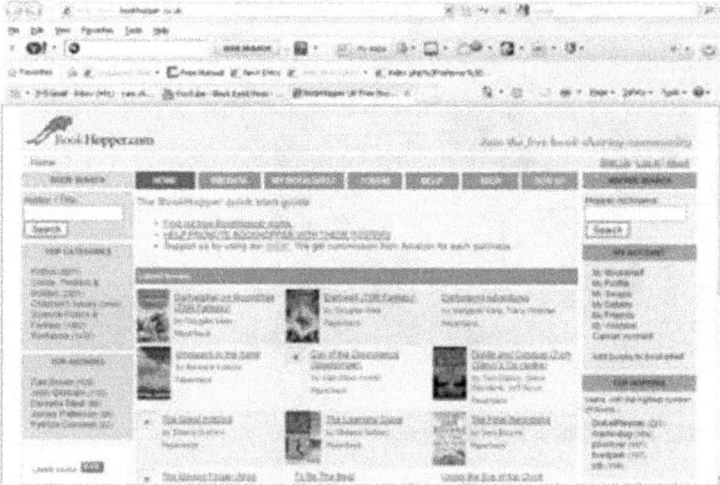

Bookins.com

This is another popular book swapping site on the web.

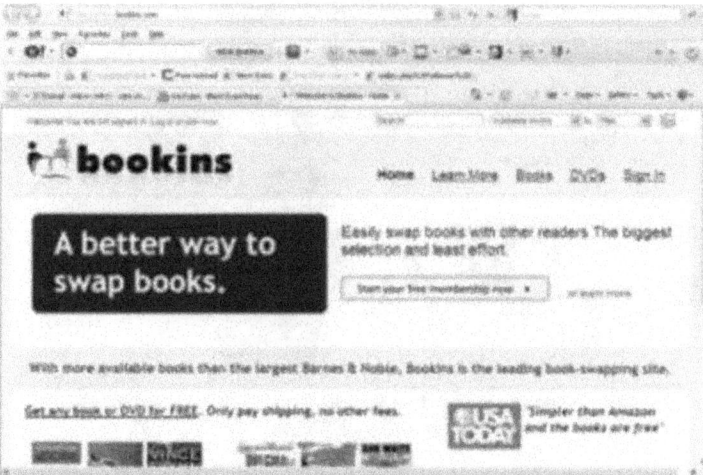

BookMooch.com

The website allows users to trade their books with each other.

BookSwim.com

This is one of the most popular book rental services on the internet.

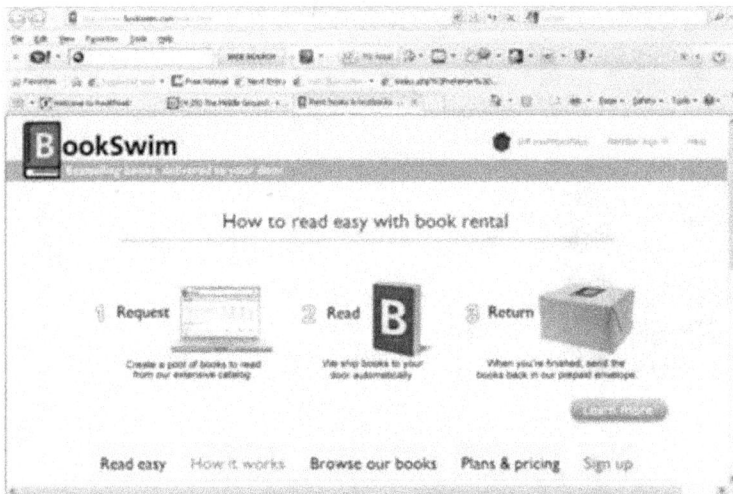

Connect Via Books.com

The site offers a platform for like minded book lovers to connect with each other.

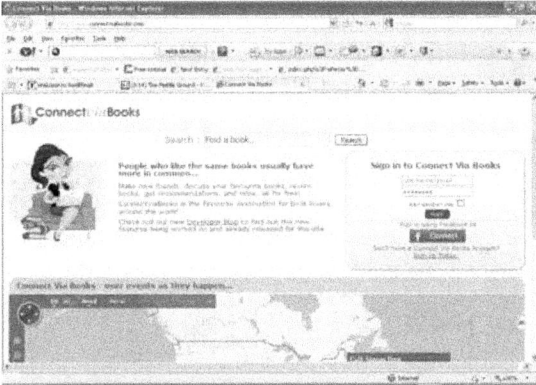

Good Reads.com

This is another great book networking site where you can connect with like minded book lovers, recommend books you have read and form book clubs.

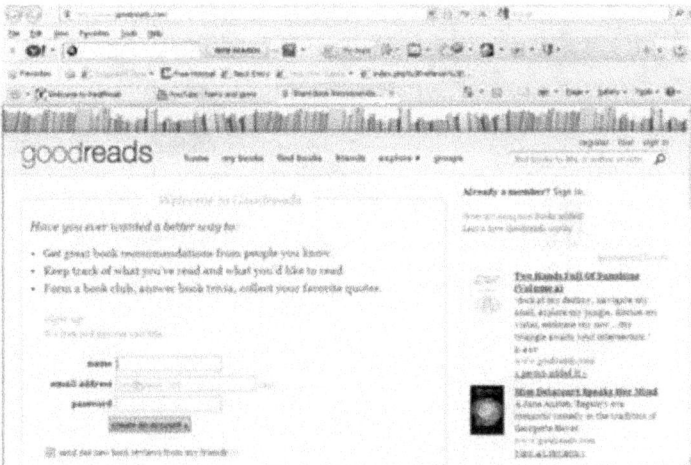

Paper Back Swap.com

As the name suggests the site allows users to trade books for free.

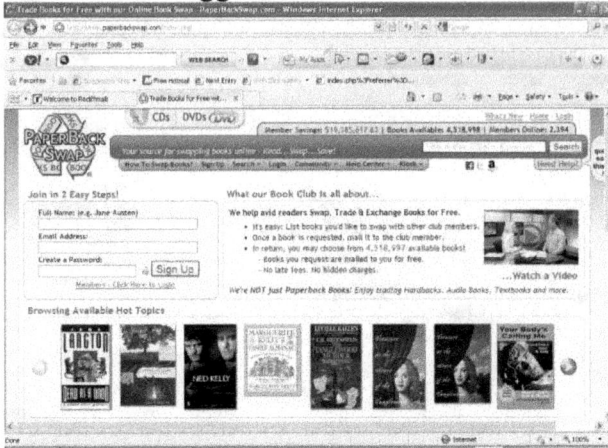

Read It Swap It.com

This is a UK based book swapping website.

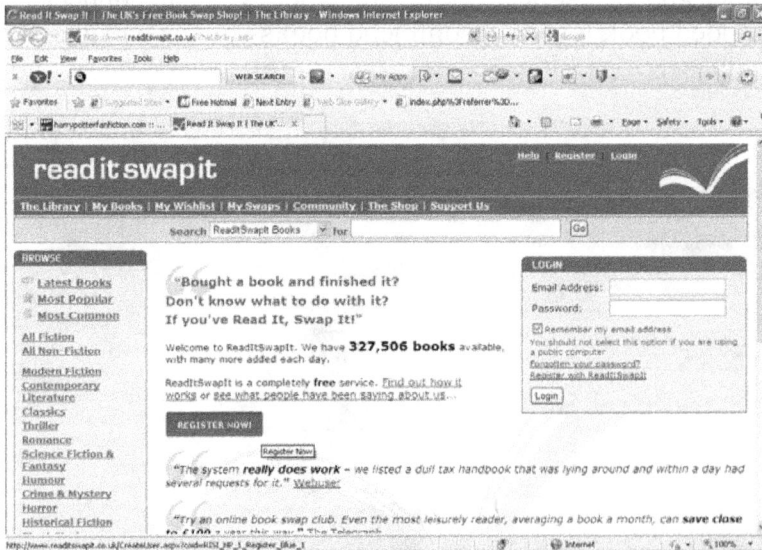

Revish.com

This is an online community for people who love reading and reviewing books.

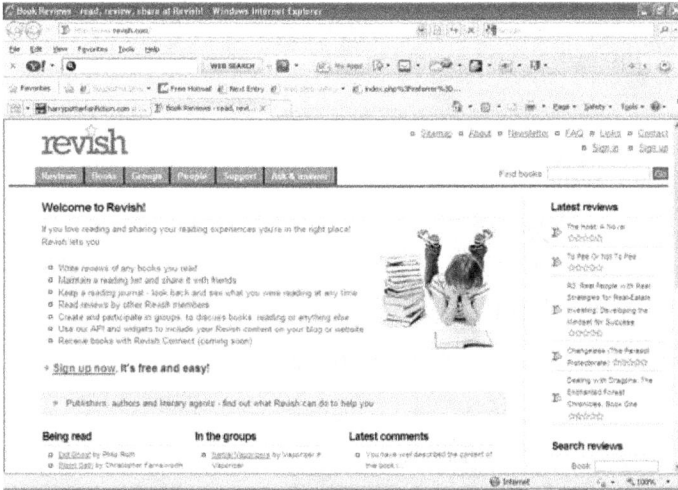

Library Thing.com

This is a social networking community of Booklovers with a user base of 1,000,000. Sign up to Library Thing is currently free.

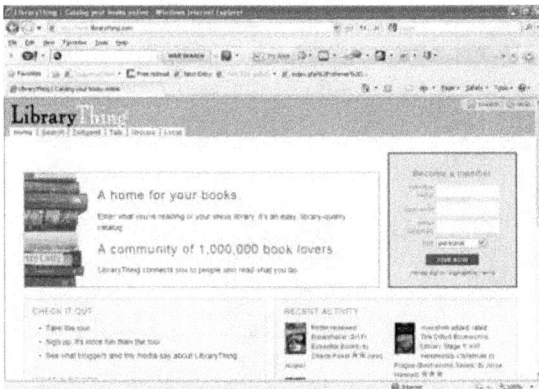

Chapter 18
Home and Family Networking Websites

These websites offer an excellent platform to marketers to connect with family based audience. This is a great market for almost all kinds of products and services. You can also expand your family contacts through these websites.

Café Mom.com

This is an online community for mothers, where they can meet share advice, make new friends and play games.

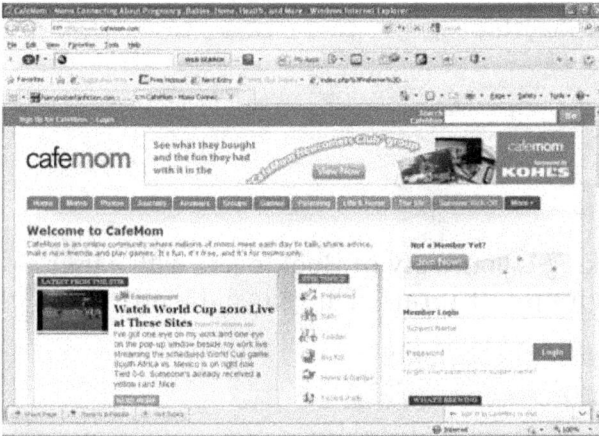

Family 2.0.com

This social networking website can help you stay connected with your family members.

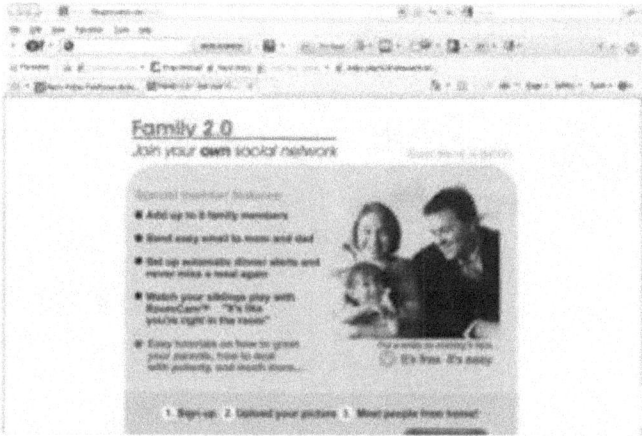

Famiva.com

This website allows families to form their own social networks.

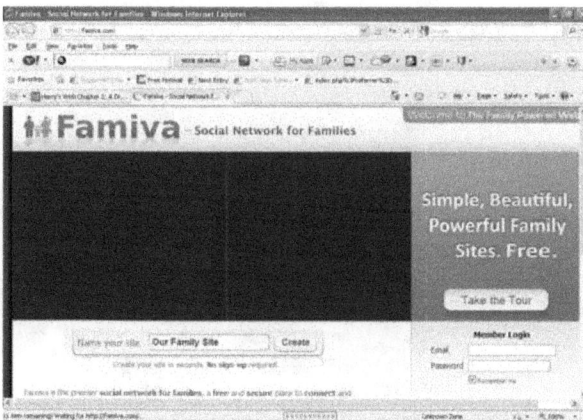

Famster.com

This website provides a platform for families to stay connected with each other.

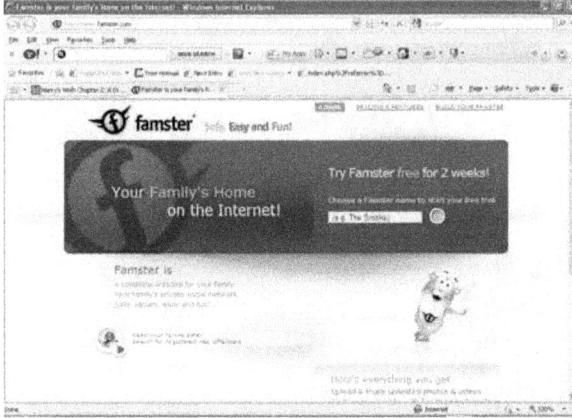

Geni.com

The website allows users to form a virtual family tree to preserve their family history and discover new relatives.

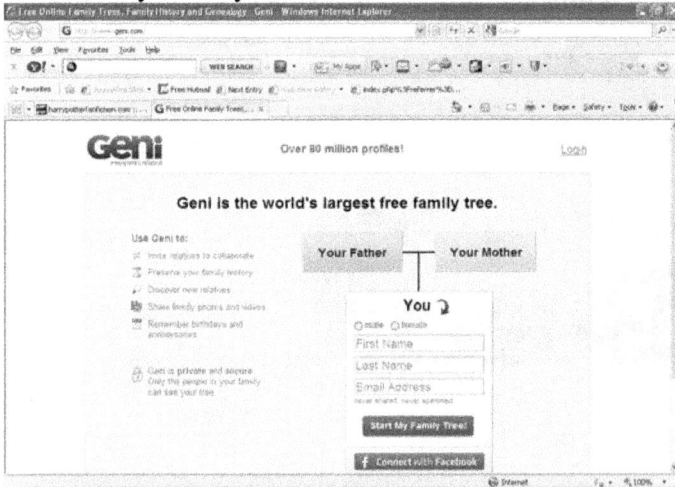

Genoom.com

This is another virtual family tree website.

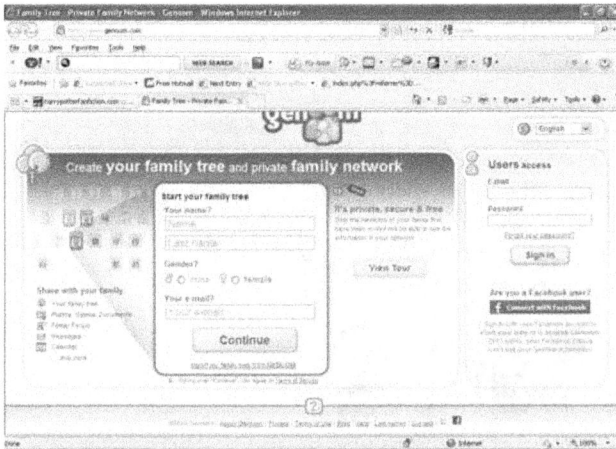

Kincafe.com

The website allows users to create their family tree, swap photos and stay connected with immediate as well as extended family.

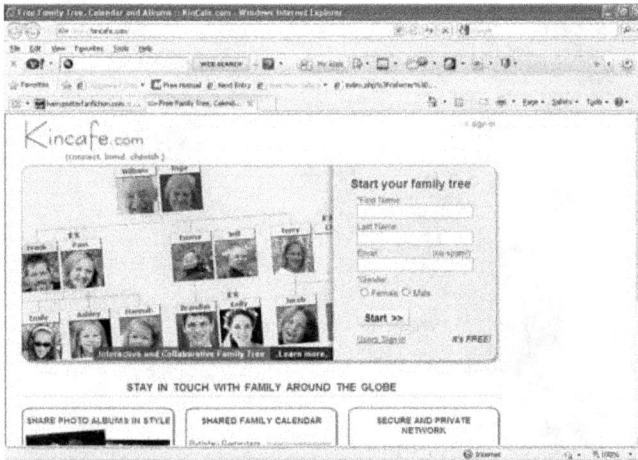

Kinzin.com

This is a social networking website that allows people to stay connected with their family members and share their photos within their closed network of family and friends.

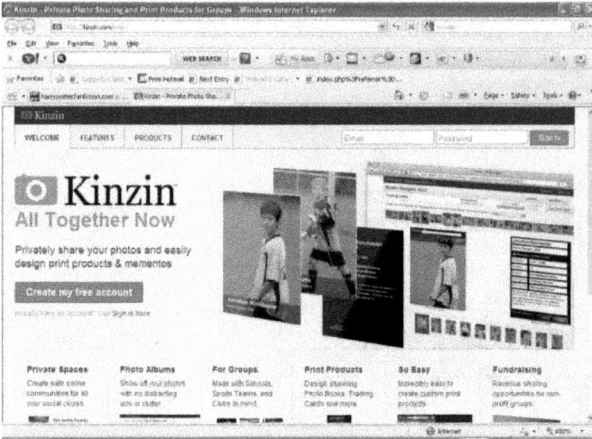

Baby Center.com

This is an online community of parents.

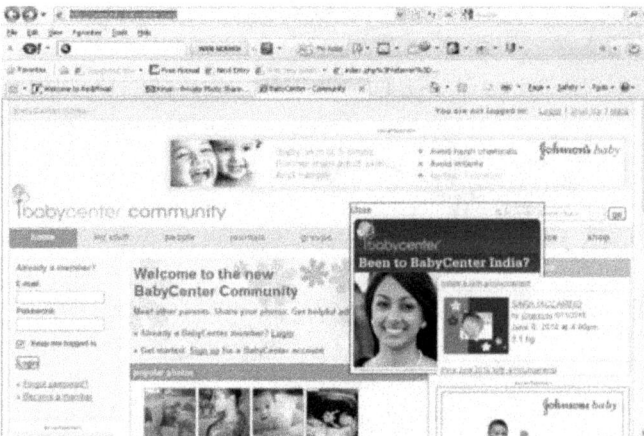

MomJunction.com

This is a great place for like minded mothers to meet and discuss their concerns and share parenting tips with each other.

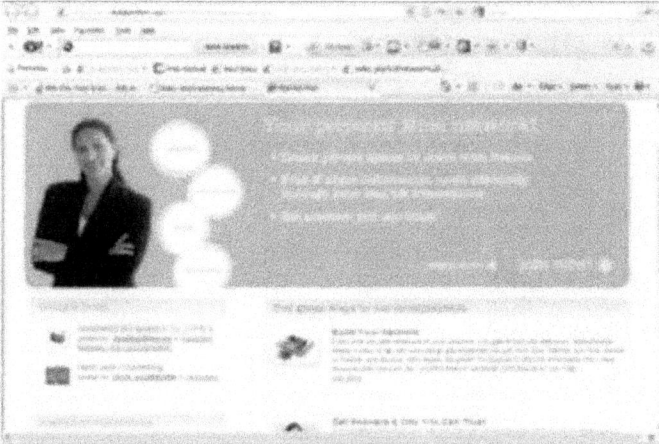

Mothers Click.com

This is a networking website for moms to connect and learn from each other.

MyFamily.com

The website provides a platform for families to share their photos, videos, have discussions and schedule events.

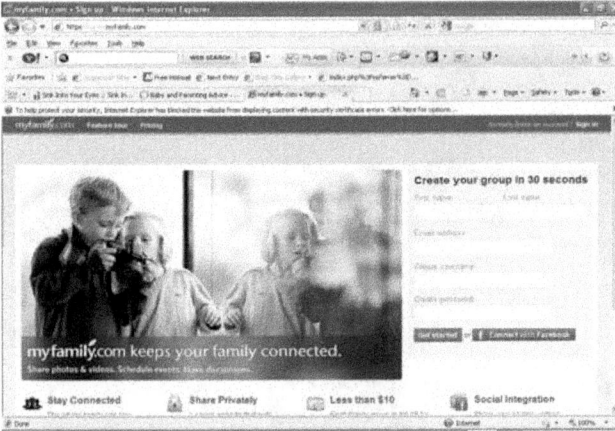

Genealogy and Family.com

The website allows users to trace their family tree and discover new relatives.

OurStory.com

The website allows families to share their anecdotes, stories, photos and videos.

The Family Post.com

This is a pay to use website that allows families to create networks of their own.

Chapter 18
Outsourcing Websites

These are the websites that will help you put your marketing plans into action! I have already discussed outsourcing websites in detail, so all I am going to say here is look through all of them carefully and select the ones that you feel will serve your needs best.

Craiglist.org

This is centralized network of online communities, featuring free online classified advertisements – with sections devoted to jobs, housing, personals, for sale, services, community, gigs, résumés, etc. The best part about Craiglist is that you simply have to click on a location and you can get in touch with providers based in that country.

Odesk.com

This is a popular outsourcing website where you can post your jobs and interview candidates for free. The website has a global user base of providers specializing in various skills including coding, website design, ghost writing, public relations, internet marketing, video editing and producing, creating podcasts, etc.

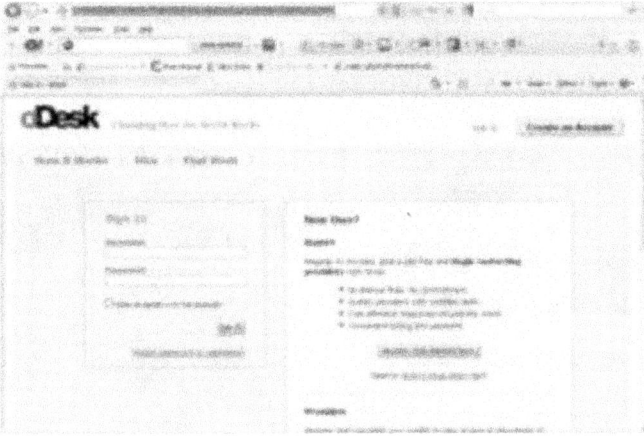

Elance.com

This is a pay to use website where you can post unlimited jobs after making a one time payment. Elance also has huge user base of providers specializing in skills like programming, marketing, writing, administration, designing, web content writing, video/audio content creation, etc.

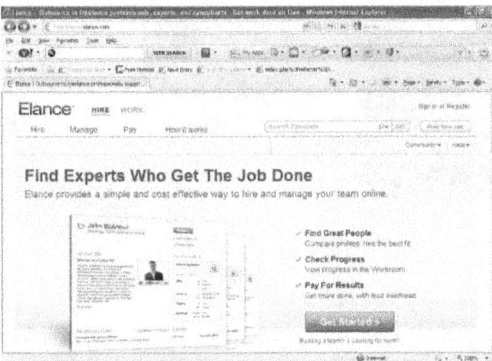

DoMyStuff.com

As the name suggests the site allows you to outsource your chores and tasks, so that you can concentrate on matters that need your complete attention. Registration to the website is currently free.

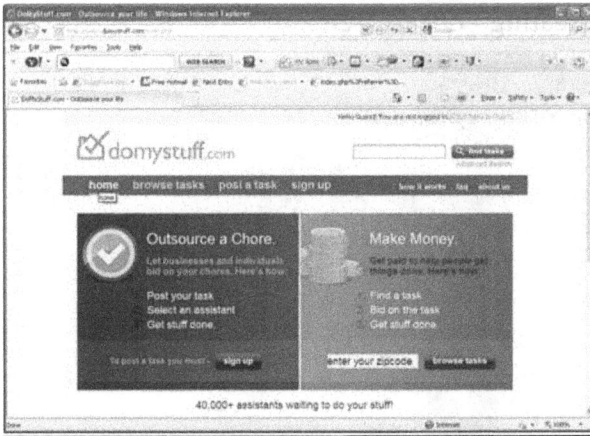

Freelancer.com

This is another outsourcing website that allows users to post their projects for free. Freelancer has huge number of registered providers from across the globe specializing in varied services like programming, administration, website design, product design, video/audio production and editing, writing, data entry, sales and marketing, etc.

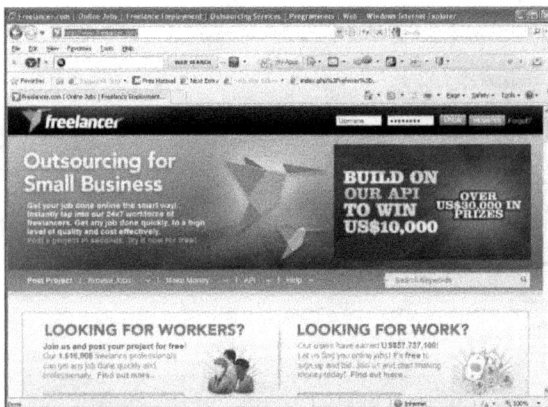

Get A Coder.com

The outsourcing website offers users a platform to tap into a global workforce of service providers like programmers, writers, web-designers, etc.

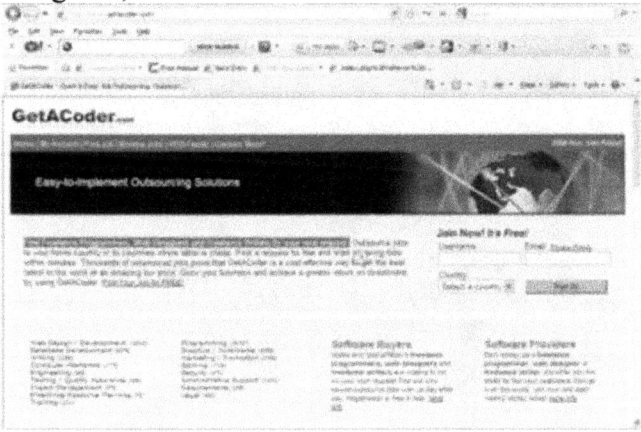

Guru.com

The website allows users to post their jobs for free. It has a huge user base of freelancers from around the world specializing in several technical and non-technical services.

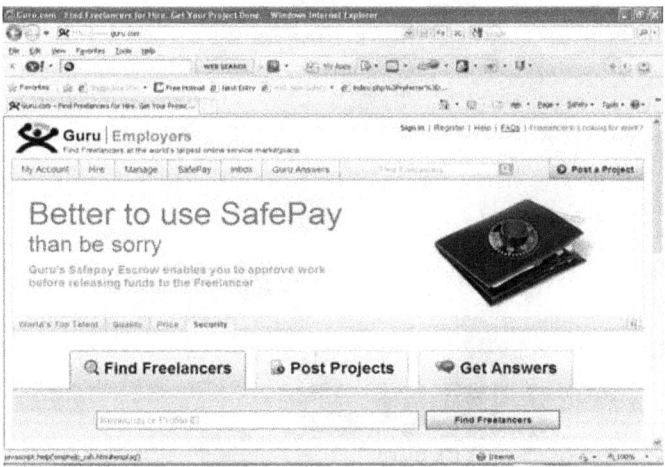

Chillibreeze.com

You can post your writing/editing/content management jobs to this site for free. The site has a user base of Indian providers.

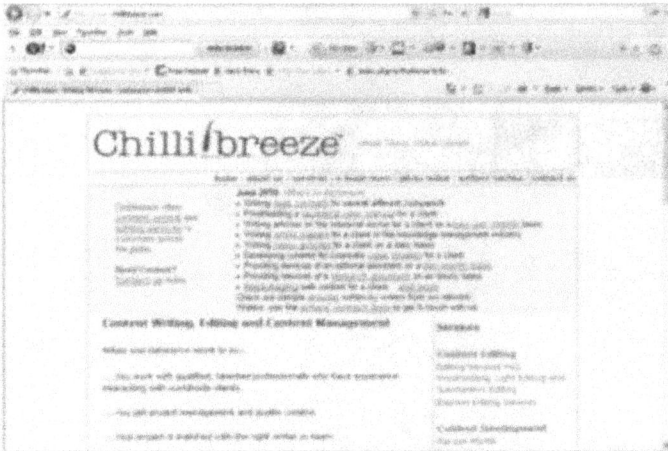

All Freelance Work.com

This is another site that allows you to outsource work to freelancers.

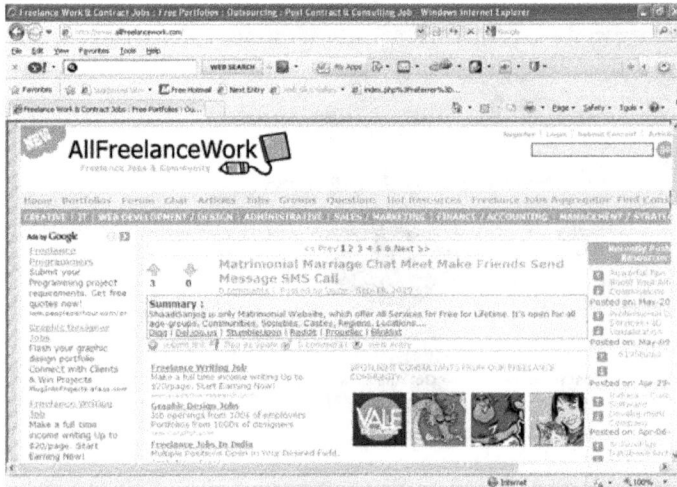

Programmingbids.com

As the name suggests the site allows you to outsource your programming and web designing jobs for free.

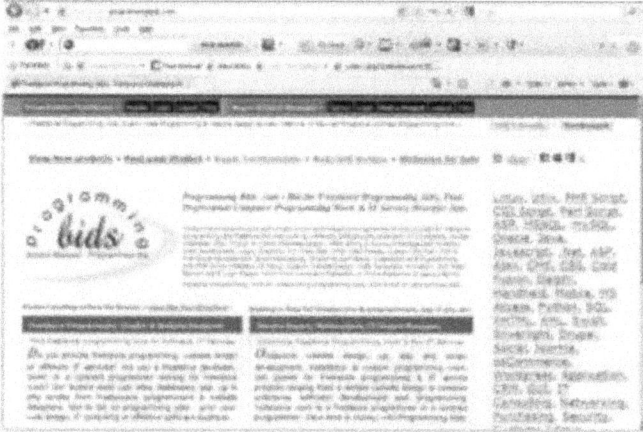

99 Designs.com

You can easily find skilled freelancers to outsource your web and logo design related jobs here, by organizing design contests through this website. The best part is that you'll get lots of options to choose from, but you only have to pay for the design you select as the winner. To post your contest you need to pay the site a hosting fee plus 15% of the prize money you offer to the winner of your contest.

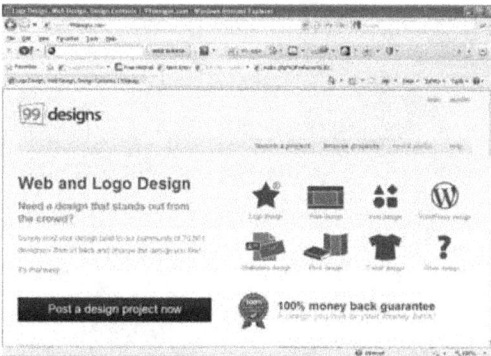

Webeserve.com

This is another website through which you can outsource all kinds of web traffic building jobs. Registration to the website is free.

Chapter 20
Conclusion

So, that was quite a long list, right? The good part is that you have finished reading through it. This means you now have all the information that you need to create an effective internet marketing campaign.

I have an included a two part appendix to help you tie in everything and put your plan into an action. These additional sections contain the information that you would need to integrate social media into your business plan.

Before you proceed to the Appendix, I would suggest that you make a list of all the websites that you feel can help you achieve your business goals. After you are done with your list, go back and read the first four chapters and then proceed to the last section of this manual.

Appendix Part-1
Additional Resources

The following is a list of resources that can help you build your online business from scratch.

Qcapacity.com

Ocapacity offers easy to use website building tools for businesses.

Kunaki.com

This is a cost effective cd/dvd manufacturing, publishing and distributing service.

1Shopping Cart.com

The pay to use service offers all the tools and solutions that your business needs to market and sell online.

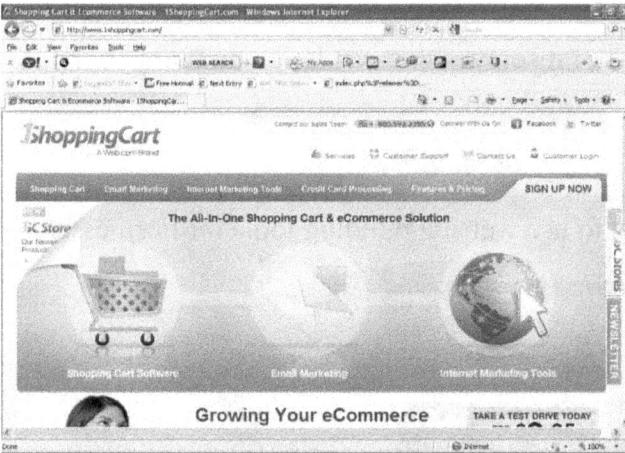

Aweber.com

This is a pay to use website that offers email marketing services.

Private label websites

You can buy original video products from these websites along with the rights to re-sell them as your own.

Source Code Goldmine

Naked Plr

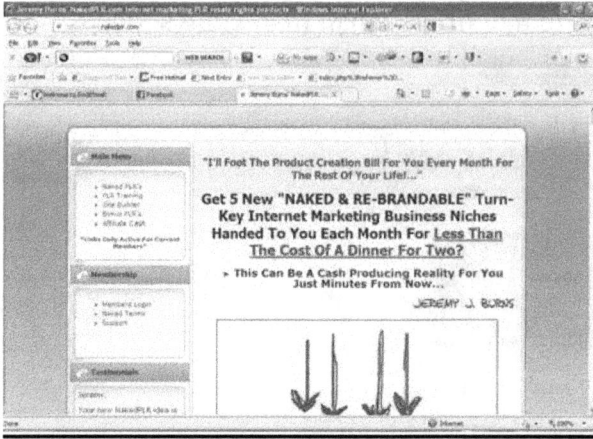

Email Marketing Manager-Profisponder

This website sells a smart mailing list and auto responder management software.

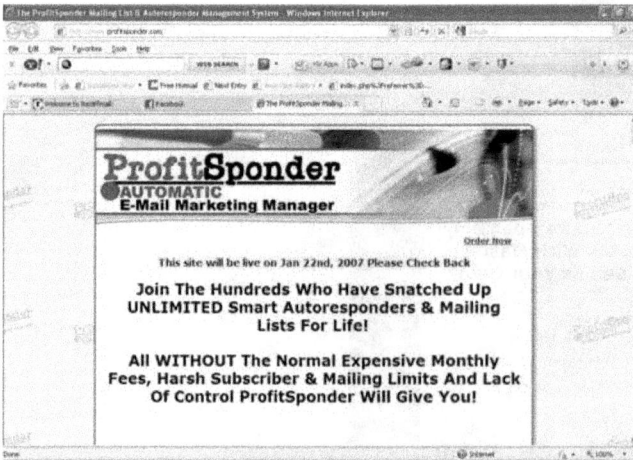

Eonline data.com

The website offers users access to the highest quality Credit Card Processing and Payment solutions.

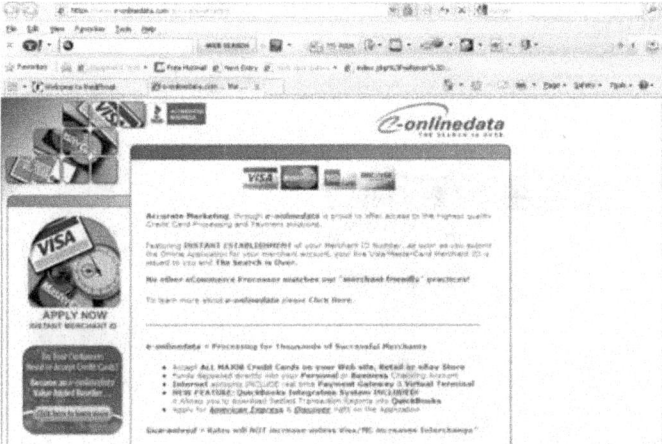

Social Oomph.com

This website can help you optimize your facebook activities.

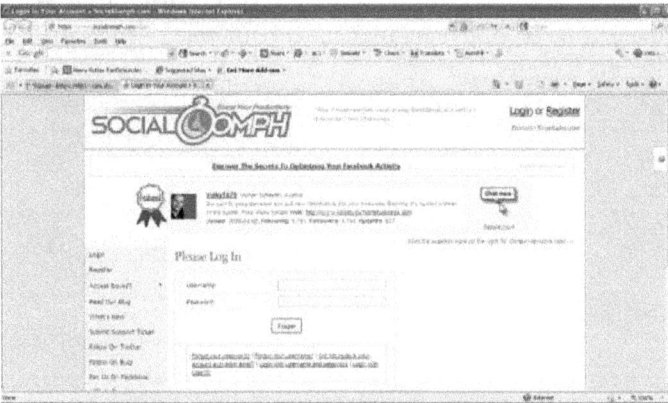

Web Marketing Magic.com

Here you can buy a tool that can help you **automate your email marketing, website sales management, digital delivery, recurring billing, credit card processing, ad tracking, affiliate program and other ecommerce activities.**

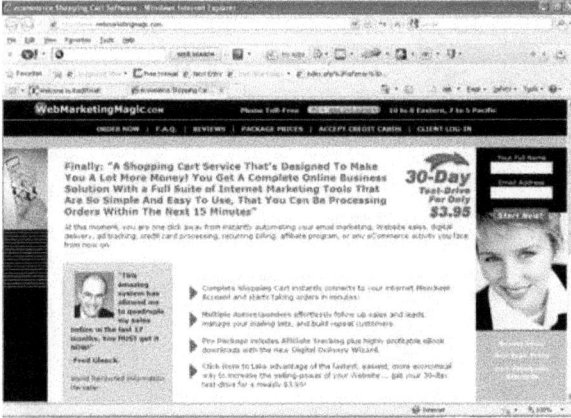

Article Directories

The following is a list of some of the best article directories that you can submit your content to in order to increase your back-links and build your online brand image.

Ezines

www.ezinearticles.com

This is one of the most popular article directories on the net and accepts only high quality content.

Go Articles.com

This directory is also quite popular and has relatively more lenient article submission guidelines.

Buzzle.com

Articles submitted here have a very good chance of being indexed by google. The site accepts only high quality content and you may have to wait for several weeks before being accepted as an author here.

ArticleDashboard.com

This article directory is easy to use and articles submitted here have a good chance of being picked up by search engines.

Article Base**.com**

You can submit your article for free here and increase your chances
of online recognition.

Press release submission directories

The following is a list of websites where you can submit your press releases for free, so that you can get more media exposure, drive more traffic to your blog and establish yourself as an authority figure in your niche area.

NPR.com

This website is a producer and distributor of noncommercial news, talk, and entertainment programming.

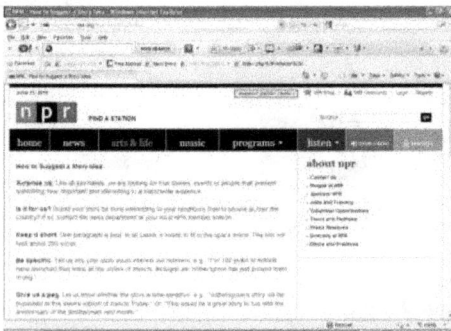

MarketWire.com

This is a newswire service that offers services like press release distribution, media contact management, media monitoring services, etc.

Pr Web.com

This is another press release distribution site that you can use to attract media coverage and build your brand image.

PR Log.com

This is a free press release submission and distribution service.

24-7 Press Release.com

This is a popular press release submission and distribution service.

Video Services.
These are resource websites that can help you get noticed through your videos.

TubeMogul.com

This is a popular video distribution service. The website allows up to 100 video deployments per month for free. Users have to pay to use the premium features that TubeMogul offers.

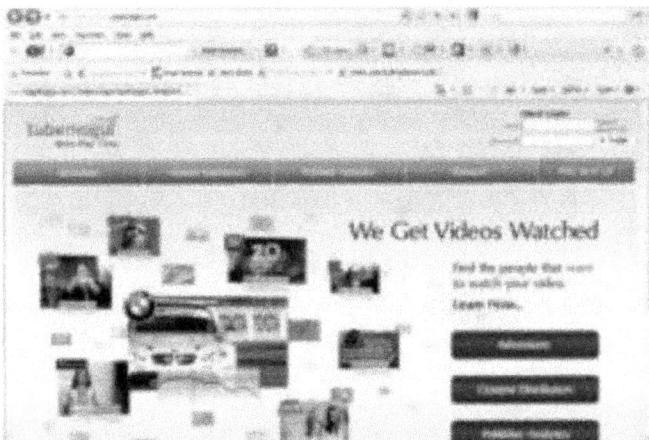

Traffic Geyser.com

The website teaches users about the power of marketing with online videos through a series of free videos and helps in distributing videos.

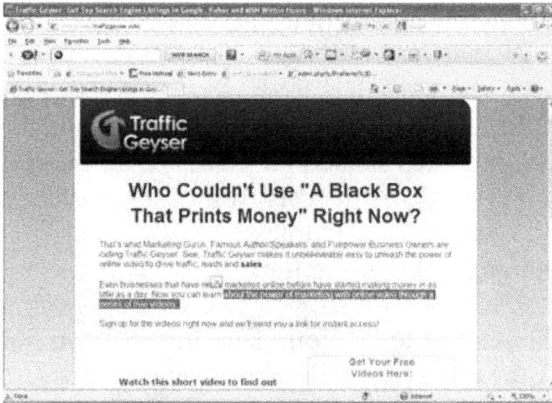

Appendix Part-2
Mobile Marketing

Wireless technology truly has revolutionized the way people stay connected. A short time ago mobile phones were seen only as accessories for well-to-do doctors and lawyers. Now they're indispensible social connections for teens, their grandparents and everyone between.

Considering that mobile phones are easier to acquire than a computer and much more user friendly, it makes sense that there are far more mobile phones in use than computers. And when something makes it easier for people to stay in contact with people and events that matter to them, it becomes engrained into the fabric of society.

Think radio, landline telephones and television. But unlike those fixed location technologies, the typical mobile phone owner keeps their mobile phone active and close to their person 24 hours per day.

So taking the time to understand how to make mobile technology work for you and your business is well worth the investment of a little bit of energy.

What Exactly is Mobile Marketing?

By now most people have been exposed to some sort of Mobile Marketing and probably have an intuitive idea of what it is, but may not be fully aware of how powerful it could be for their business.

Mobile marketing is defined by the Mobile Marketing Association as *"a set of practices that enables organizations to communicate and engage with their audience in an interactive and relevant manner through any mobile device or network."*

No matter how it's defined, what it means for your business is person, instant and responsive contact with your customers no matter where they are.
SMS messaging is by far the most widely available platforms for mobile marketing and is usually the first to come to mind.

SMS is the acronym for Short Message Service and is the industry name for those plain text 160 character messages.

i.e. TEXT 'ABCDE' to "12345" to [vote, donate, receive your FREE GIFT, etc]

From the $5 prepaid drug store phone to the $2000 Doohickey Supreme phone, just about every operational mobile phone can send and receive SMS Messages.
SMS mobile marketing and can work for any customer focused business. Not only is this platform universal but when compared to other forms of mobile marketing can offer the best ROI.

If you are sure of your target market's mobile technological savvy, your marketing options open up quite a bit.   There is also the MMS platform (Multimedia Messaging Service).

If your product appeals to the senses in any way, MMS messaging may be a better option for you because this is the platform used for picture and video messages. As many mobile users will forward a funny video or picture message faster than email this can be an excellent marketing tool for viral messages.

For example, Domino's pizza is currently asking their customers to take pictures of their pizzas and submit them. This is an ingenious idea, for those customers who take the picture with there cell phones, Dominos is making use of MMS mobile marketing without the customer even realizing that he's being marketed to.

For those customers who use a digital camera and upload the pictures they've just volunteered to be on the list without Dominos having to offer anything.
Since the customer has already purchased the pizza they have less resistance towards participating. This is almost as ingenious as their 1980's campaign of 30 minutes or less or it's free.

While in 2008 it was estimated that there were 1.3 billion MMS users, keep in mind that not all phones have this capability.

Technology is moving faster than manufacturers and the networks can keep up and there are many compatibility gaps. For example only in the last 3 years has RIM (Research in Motion the manufacturers of Blackberry) realized that people desire to use their Blackberries for more than work.

In an effort to regain the smart phone market share lost to the iPhone and Droid there has been an onslaught of new mobile service rich smart phones.
Great for all those new converts but unfortunate for anyone with a Blackberry manufactured before December 2007.

As they're unable to access many of these newer interactive features. In fact, some Blackberries manufactured as late as 2008 can not access MMS capabilities on some networks.
So unless you are sure of the mobile technological savvy of your end user or you just don't mind leaving some customers out in the cold SMS is the best way to go. Texting has become so prevalent that many municipalities have enacted texting while driving laws to curb the wanton messaging in dangerous situations.

What Businesses are Best Suited for Mobile Marketing?

Hello (tap...tap...tap) have you been listening?
Just about everyone has a cell phone. In most metropolitan areas they can be purchased where laundry detergent is sold and in some cases for less money. So unless your target audience consists of 90 year old invalids in rest homes every business can benefit from a well designed mobile marketing strategy.

I'm sure you've know of some of the other well known companies such as Amazon, Google, eBay and Facebook that are utilizing mobile technology to connect with their users.

But what about the regular guy?
The one whose pockets are not IPO billions deep.

During these economic lean years when every marketing dollar has to count, it's the regular guy who can reap the most benefits from implementing a mobile marketing strategy. As of right now mobile devices are considered very personal. Your customer may have to share his computer with other members of the household or community, but for most people their mobile phone is very private and messages received are viewed as being more personal than other types of communication. This places your message in a better position to be viewed and acted upon.

One of the most important factors about the rapidly exploding mobile trend is that traditional, long-standing demographics are out the window. Granny has a cell phone and she knows how to use it. We need to approach mobile marketing with fresh eyes and open minds.

Ways to implement mobile technology into your marketing strategy Mobilize your Site

One of the simple and low cost ways to implement mobile marketing is to create a mobile version of your site. What's the use of spending the money to entice your customer via a mobile device only to wait until he/she reaches a computer to make the sale or capture the lead? Make every attempt to hold your customer's attention for as long as possible and it's not as difficult as you may think.

With today's Mobile browsers like Opera Mini and WindowsCE many sites render visually almost as good as the original. However much interactivity is lost and some designs just won't scale.
But there are solutions.

Let's look how we at Baltimore REI are utilizing mobile marketing to promote our message and develop our customer relationships.

.mobi is a top level domain dedicated to mobile web browsers however simply recreating your site with a .mobi extension does not necessarily mean your site will reproduce a mini-version of itself. We discuss more about marketing with your own Short code at the end of this chapter

To maximize the benefit of your mobile optimized site. Keep it simple. Pare your site down to the absolute need to know. Remember that some people pay heavily for each megabyte downloaded on their mobiles (not to mention for the time)... and they're not going to wait twenty minutes for all your graphics and plug-ins to load.

- First of all we're using regular SMS and Short Codes to ensure that technology doesn't become a hindrance to response.

- We've provided a good incentive to join.

- We've also created a mobile device friendly site. http://www.baltimorereia.mobi as a companion to our main site http://www.baltimorereia.com

Regardless of your business type this strategy works, 3 days we received over 60 Opt-Ins and it was a lot of fun…

If you run (or will consider) running your site on the Wordpress blog platform, creating a mobile friendly site is as easy as installing the superb and very user-friendly plug in WordPress Mobile edition. If you can't find it by searching the plug-in section via your blog Dashboard, you can easily download it from WordPress.org's plug-in section.

Other than the easy installation, this plug-in will automatically detect a mobile user and direct them to the mobile device optimized site. This can be very helpful for users who are unfamiliar with the .mobi extension.

MobilePress.com

If you'd rather customize your blog theme somewhat, a plug-in you may like is MobilePress. This one isn't available at WordPress.org, but you can find it on its home site, mobilepress.co.za.

Customize your themes: it also allows specific themes for the iPhone, as well as the Opera Mini browser and Windows CE Mobile. (Surprisingly simple to install!)

Mobilestoremaker.com

If you have an e-store, making it mobile-accessible is an absolute essential. This tool allows for you to sell your wares directly through your customer's mobile phone. Imagine how powerful this could be. Your customer sees your ad while sitting in the doctor's office. Normally she would have to clip your ad and remember to visit your site when she got home. However with your mobile store information she can complete the purchase while she waits. Instantly

Mobilize your Downloads

If you sell digital material mobilize it.
Adobe .pdf has become the industry standard for downloadable ebooks and courses however since the iPad is still so new many sellers do not realize that the device can read those Acrobat pdfs just the same as the Mac. Considering that 45,000 iPads sold in the first 2 hours and 300,000 iPads were sold on the first day, don't sleep on this market. If you're producing digital .pdf's, make sure you tell your iPad visitors that your e-book is viewable on their iPads.

Mobipocket Creator allows you to convert your digital files into .mobi format. With the free reader software, this format is readable by most smart phones and the Kindle. This format offers better DRM (Digital Rights Management) than Acrobat as well.

Mobilize your Reach

I've covered many different ways you can make your site and products more mobile device friendly. Now let's talk a bit about how to get these mobile users in your snares in the first place.

As tempting as it may be you can not simply grab your list of customer mobile numbers and start sending messages and links. You must respect the same rules of permission based marketing as with email.

The easiest way is to make them raise their hand and ask to participate. (Remember the Domino's pizza MMS marketing strategy?)
First of all, how well do you know your target customer? What do they want from you that you can utilize to create a win-win situation? This may come in the form of discount codes, free samples, motivational quotes, industry tips or the chance to provide input.

The best way to start creating your mobile marketing plan is to think about what your customer buys from you normally and figure out how to make it easier for them to get if they opt-in.

To ensure that your customer has several opportunities to see your opt-in message place the information prominently on your:

✓ Website
✓ Signage
✓ Marketing materials
✓ On Hold Message/ Voice Mail Message
✓ Emails/Email signatures
✓ Advertising
✓ Billboards
✓ Social Networking
✓ Everywhere you Market

As I stated earlier mobile devices are viewed much more personally than email so always be respectful of your customer. You must create a compelling reason for your customer to give you their phone number but as with email marketing some of the most common enticers are:

❖ A Chance to win a big prize
❖ Something FREE
❖ Voting (This can be for anything- Vote YES or NO Did you really think Brett Favre would retire or Vote YES or NO should Cleveland still be angry at Baltimore about the Ravens?)
❖ What they want

➢ Location-specific Information
➢ Timely knowledge
➢ Financial Incentive
➢ Make life easier
➢ Entertainment
➢ Connection

How to get started?

A lot of examples of mobile marketing strategies have been provided however the easiest and the fastest way to out the gate is the plain text 160 character SMS message.

TEXT 'ABCDE' to "12345" to [vote, donate, receive your FREE GIFT, etc]

A SMS marketing Opt-in text consists of two parts the Short Code which is the 5-6 digit number that the message is sent to and the Keyword - Which is the first word of the text and triggers the software application return a message, record the senders phone number etc.

Seeing as the cost for leasing a private Short Code is about $500 per month (Common Short Code Administration) most marketers find it easier to utilize a SMS vendor. These vendors allow marketers to share short codes for an economical monthly/message fee.

To help decide if a vendor will meet your needs consider the following:

1. Is the company stable and does it serve your target area?
2. Do they support the major cellular carriers?
3. SAFETY (must focus on permission!)
4. Offer any Specialty Services you may require (MMS, attachments)
5. Campaign Types offered
6. Interface/Opt-In methods
7. Customer Service Access
8. Price/Reseller Program

There are several cost effective companies that can provide immediate access to short codes for your campaign.

Protexting.com

Probably one of the most cost effective SMS vendor available for newbies.

EZ Texting.com

Very popular, reliable and user friendly.

Popular and all inclusive specialty plans like mobile voting ready to go out the box.

Mobile marketing is a sleeping giant that any success minded entrepreneur would be remiss to ignore. And if you can get past the misconception that it's only suitable for "techie" businesses or that it's going to burden you with more work, you will find a whole new window of opportunity for customer relationship building.

Mobile technology has simplified life for thousands of people; taking away some of the technological stress brought by computer domination and allows people who've never thought of themselves as technologically savvy to participate.

Advertise
Identify the websites from this book through which you can reach your target customers, get in touch with advertising departments of your selected sites and then buy their web space to place sticky ads or pay per click ads promoting your business/website. You can also look at some classified ad posting communities and journals, if you think they can help you reach out to your target market.

E-mail Campaigns and Press releases
Drafting persuasive newsletters, e-mails detailing offers or citing information that may be of use to your subscribers can help you increase your brand re-call value. Striking cross-promoting deals with other businesses can also help you expand your customer base. You can find businesses to partner with easily through business and social networking websites. Following up the e-mail newsletters with a monthly call can help you convert interested subscribers into customers.

Join Social Networking Communities
As I have mentioned earlier joining social networking communities that are closest to your niche area and have a user base that fits your target market can help you build your brand value and customer base. However, you must remember not to violate the TOS of these communities and avoid making your posts or comments overtly promotional.

Social Bookmarking
Simply building your profile on social bookmarking sites and bookmarking your own content won't get you traffic. The key to success through social bookmarking lies in creating great content and making it easy for users to bookmark your pages by placing bookmarking widgets on your web page.

I have already discussed some dos and don'ts of content creation in the chapter on social bookmarking, so keep those rules in mind and you will get bookmarked on your own. Creating content for Wikipedia as I mentioned earlier is also a great way to get bookmarked.

Video sharing and Podcasts

This marketing strategy will get you very far if you do it right. You can upload reality style interesting and informational videos related to your business or record customer testimonials in the form of interviews and upload them on video sharing websites. For this purpose in fact you can also use video distribution services offered at extremely reasonable prices by several online companies.

 I have a mentioned a few Appendix one.
Converting some of your articles and blogs into podcasts and posting them on relevant sites can help you reach those people who prefer listening to reading.

Press releases and wires
There are several free online press release distribution services on the net. Make good use of them to attract media attention. Having your business's name mentioned in a positive light in news and media publications can help you generate a lot of goodwill.

Install Google Analytics and subscribe to weekly traffic reports
Monitoring your traffic on a weekly basis will help you identify whether or not your social marketing campaign is working for you. These reports also detail the source of the hits, so you will be able to identify exactly which platforms are serving as high traffic generators.

The **diagram** below indicates a marketing strategy based on the points I have mentioned above-

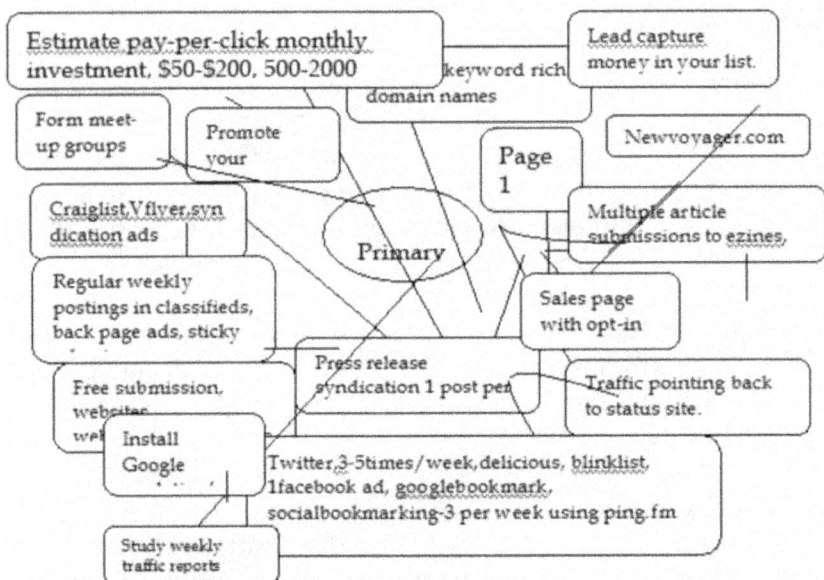

Estimate pay-per-click monthly investment, $50-$200, 500-2000

keyword rich domain names

Lead capture money in your list.

Form meet-up groups

Promote your

Page 1

Newvoyager.com

Craiglist,V flyer,syndication ads

Primary

Multiple article submissions to ezines,

Regular weekly postings in classifieds, back page ads, sticky

Sales page with opt-in

Free submission, websites

Press release syndication 1 post per

Traffic pointing back to status site.

Install Google

Twitter,3-5times/week,delicious, blinklist, 1facebook ad, googlebookmark, socialbookmarking-3 per week using ping.fm

Study weekly traffic reports

I have made this diagram in the Link wheel format so that you can comprehend it easily. This diagram is just an example of a marketing strategy that you can adopt; you can of course make changes to it based on your needs, budget, business type and comfort level.

For instance, if you cannot afford to make videos, you may consider increasing your article directory submissions or you may prefer posting sticky ads to classifieds. The permutations and combinations are endless.

So, get to work and start planning your marketing strategy.

Good Luck.
See you on the other side of success!

THE MASTERMIND SOLUTION
Series
.com

Henry Lawrence
Three Super Bowl
Championship Rings

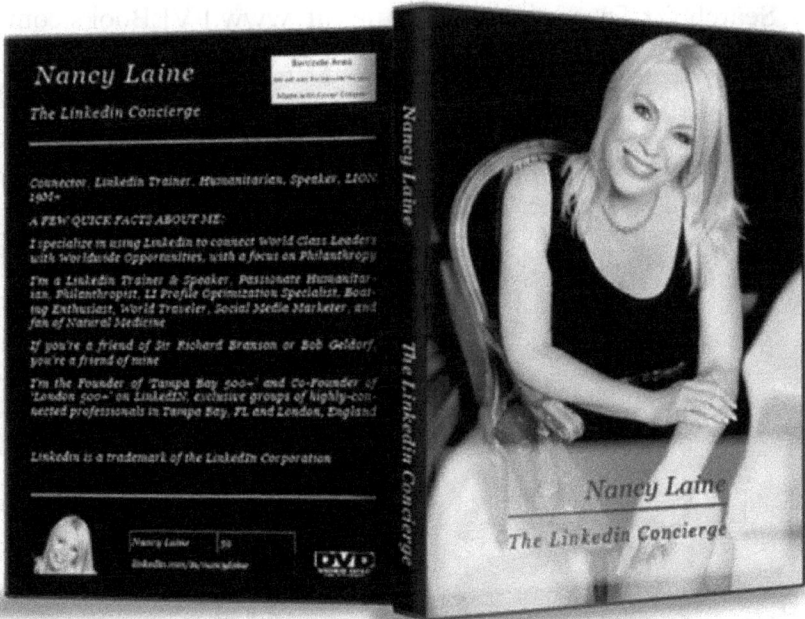

Amazon Short Direct Link **http://dld.bz/bHGJ5**

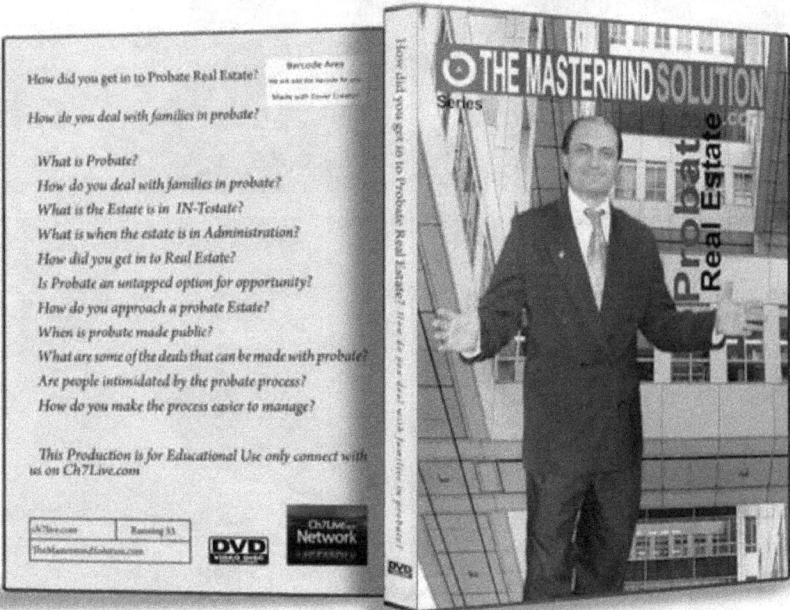

Amazon Short Direct Link **http://dld.bz/bHGUh**

www.ingramcontent.com/pod-product-compliance
Lightning Source LLC
Chambersburg PA
CBHW072303210326
41519CB00057B/2608